THREE
INGREDIENT
BAKING

THREE INGREDIENT BAKING

SARAH RAINEY

MICHAEL JOSEPH
an imprint of
PENGUIN BOOKS

CONTENTS

INTRODUCTION

How is that even POSSIBLE? I'm hoping that's the thought that's going through your head right now. What on earth can you bake using only three ingredients?

Most of you probably picked this book up out of curiosity – or complete and utter disbelief. If you were given it as a present, someone clearly thought you'd be intrigued. Either way, I bet you're wondering what's coming next. So, let me start by introducing myself.

My name is Sarah and I love to bake. I'm not a professional chef, I don't run a cake shop and I've never appeared on *The Great British Bake Off* – although I wish all three of those things were true. Nope, I'm just a writer, whose passions in life are scribbling about food, baking at all hours of the day and night and eating pretty much everything I lay my eyes on.

I've been baking since I was a toddler, flour-caked hands tugging on apron strings in my grandma's tiny kitchen in Northern Ireland where I grew up. Grandma Arthur – Kay, she was called – is the reason I bake. She made scones so good they could make you cry, cakes that were fluffier than a cloud, buttery biscuits that melted in your mouth.

She taught my mum, another brilliant baker, who honed her skills at Le Cordon Bleu cookery school (the same place that trained the late, great Julia Child) and brought me, my sister and my brother up on hearty, home-cooked food.

As for me? My only real claim to baking fame is that I once made a cake for Mary Berry – and she said it tasted 'pretty good'. So why have I written a cookery book? Well, let me take you into the weird and wonderful world of three-ingredient baking – and I guarantee you'll be as hooked as I am . . .

*'Three-ingredient baking harks back to the
cookery customs of the past: mouthwatering, nourishing,
comforting goodies whose taste isn't compromised by
counting calories or cutting out sugar.'*

Step back in time to 2013, when a Japanese food blogger called Ochikeron (whose name translates as 'hilarious') uploaded a video for three-ingredient baked cheesecake – a simple dessert made from eggs, white chocolate and cream cheese – to her YouTube channel.

Without the conventional ingredients (no butter, sugar or flour), it didn't sound like it would work, and if it did turn into something resembling a cheesecake, surely it couldn't taste like one? But Ochikeron proved us all wrong.

Viewers tested her recipe and were flabbergasted. It didn't just 'work'; the cheesecake was downright delicious. The video went viral, racking up eight million views – and turning Ochikeron into a culinary sensation overnight.

From the moment I saw that video, I was obsessed. If you could make a cheesecake – by no means an easy dessert – from just three everyday ingredients, what else could you whip up from a few things stashed away in the back of your fridge?

I started scouring every recipe book, website and Instagram page I could find for three-ingredient baking ideas. I looked into the history of three-ingredient baking, which dates back as far as rationing in Britain in the forties, and spans as far afield as Africa, Asia and Australia. Ingenious home chefs, it seems, have been looking for shortcuts for decades, swapping standard baking ingredients for clever substitutes that do the job of several – and taste better than one.

I came across scones made from lemonade, biscuits from peanut butter, cakes made from chocolate milk and crêpes from cauliflower. I rummaged in the attic and found old family recipes for shortbread and potato farls, Mars bar sauce and soda bread. I rediscovered my favourite ways of making fudge, toffee, honeycomb and macaroons.

I magicked muffins out of ginger beer, mousse out of water, ice lollies out of sherbet. I lived, breathed and ate three-ingredient baking, fed it to my very patient husband for almost every meal and plied my family, friends and colleagues with it.

For almost two years, I went on a journey – one of love, laughter and most certainly lbs. I wrote hundreds of recipes, tested them repeatedly, adapted them and adopted some I found along the way. And I put all the important lessons I learned between the covers of this book . . .

First, modern recipes tend to include an awful lot of ingredients. If you're a novice baker, not a baker at all or you simply don't have all day to make a Victoria sponge, it's pretty off-putting to pick up a recipe containing 27 obscure and expensive ingredients, most of which you can't pronounce, let alone find on the shelves of your local supermarket.

This book is, as the name suggests, the exact opposite. I've been really strict on this: each recipe contains exactly three ingredients, no more and no fewer. There's no extra seasoning, fiddly decorations or hidden extras; even water counts. There are serving suggestions, sure, but most of these are swaps – and not annoying additions. So if you're reading this feeling a little overwhelmed by baking, I promise this book is as un-scary as it gets.

Second, most of these recipes are quick and easy to make. There are a couple that take a little more time (like my 'slow and steady banana bread' – but that's sort of in the name) and you'll need to know a few basic techniques, like whisking and folding, but beyond that, it really is straightforward. They're perfect for children, adults, experts, amateurs, students, first-timers, old-timers – anyone, really, who wants to give three-ingredient baking a go.

Third, this is not – and I cannot emphasize it enough – a healthy baking book. If you want chia seeds, cacao nibs and lashings of avocado, look away now. Yes, some of my recipes are low in sugar, gluten-free and 'raw' – but I'm making no claims about their health benefits or nutritional value. There's more than enough of that to go around in the food world right now.

In my eyes, baking is an indulgence; it's not something you should eat all the time, nor is it something you should consume in huge quantities (though I do find this second part tricky). It's a gooey, sticky, stodgy, oozy luxury – and that's what this book is all about.

I might as well admit it now: my brownie recipe contains a whole jar of Nutella. I use an entire packet of buttery, calorie-laden pains au chocolat doused in cream to make a pudding. And don't even get me started on the fat content of my Oreo fudge.

So, if that sounds like your sort of thing, you've come to the right place. Three-ingredient baking harks back to the cookery customs of the past: mouthwatering, nourishing, comforting goodies whose taste isn't compromised by counting calories or cutting out sugar. But that doesn't make it old-fashioned. Because at the same time, it's convenient, efficient and good value for money – perfect for busy people on a budget, students or anyone trying to feed a young family.

I am indebted to the many food bloggers, YouTubers and recipe authors whose brilliant baking ideas have inspired and instructed me while writing this book. I credit you all with reigniting my love of baking and with reminding me that it is an alchemy like no other, in which unassuming raw ingredients are transformed into things of beauty. Any bursts of creativity in here I dedicate to you; all the mistakes are mine alone.

Before you get started, I'll leave you with this thought. Three, it is often said, is a magic number. So use this book to rediscover what that means. Try new things. Experiment. Get your hands dirty. Make mistakes. Sift flour all over your kitchen floor and get bread dough stuck to the ceiling. Bake with friends. Bake for friends. Bake first thing in the morning and in the middle of the night. Be bold. Be hungry. Make people happy.

And most important of all: make magic.

Sarah Rainey
March 2018

HANDY HINTS

Here are a few bits of general housekeeping to read before you get stuck in. If you have any questions, queries or moments of panic mid-recipe, chances are the answer's in here . . .

Oven temperature

My oven's a funny old beast. It only has three settings – fan, grill or off – which makes it just about impossible to bake things in, unless you've spent several years getting to know its weird ways. Thankfully, I have. Provided here are temperatures for both fan and normal ovens, but you may need to adjust timings to suit your particular oven.

Spoonfuls

All chefs have different interpretations of the word 'teaspoon' or 'tablespoon'. Some like them heaped, others level; others still use confusing words like 'generous' or 'rounded'. When one of my recipes calls for a spoonful, it means just that: stick the spoon in the jar, take out a measure of whatever it is, and don't worry too much about the exact size.

Eggs, bananas, etc.

Nature doesn't make things to order, which can be a pain when a recipe calls for a 'large' egg or a 'small' banana. So don't worry. I've used medium eggs throughout, and the fruit and veg are just average, normal-sized pieces of food – it won't ruin the recipe if yours is a few centimetres out.

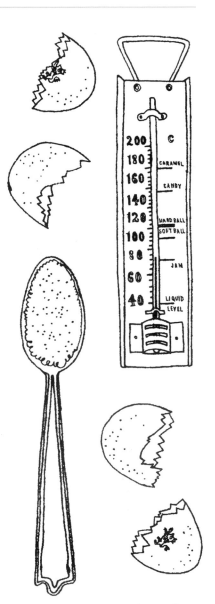

Timing

I've designed these recipes to be as quick and easy as possible. But do have a quick scan of the method before you start to check how long each one is going to take. Some of the ice creams, breads and even the biscuits have freezing, resting or setting stages before they're ready to eat – many of them overnight – and I don't want you getting hungry.

Butter

Bakers tend to go for unsalted butter, as it doesn't add flavour or take away the sweetness with a big punch of salt. But if your house is anything like mine, you'll tend to have salted butter in the fridge – as it's the one that tastes best lathered on a big hunk of crusty bread. So unless a recipe specifically calls for salted or unsalted butter, use whichever you have to hand – in fact, salted tends to be better, as it gives you two flavours in one. My go-to is Kerrygold Irish butter, as it's the saltiest of the lot – but you might prefer a different brand.

Microwaving

Like my oven, my 'category D' micro-wave is a little bit special (read: temperamental and unpredictable). If you're cooking something in the micro-wave, don't stick rigidly to the time in the recipe: watch it through the little window and heat it in short bursts.

Size

In the world of baking, size does matter. I've divided my various trays and tins into different sizes and listed their dimensions in the 'kitchen tools' section for you to refer to. But there are plenty of ways to get around it if you don't have the right one. Lakeland sells a snazzy 'multisize cake pan', which you can split into different shapes and sizes using removable dividers – or you can do it the old-fashioned way and make a fake 'edge' out of folded foil.

Lining your tin

Most recipes start with the words 'Grease and line the tin'. All this means is swab the insides with a layer of butter or neutral oil (olive oil has quite a strong flavour, so if you don't have any butter, use vegetable or sunflower oil), cut some greaseproof paper to fit and stick this on the base and sides so the cake/loaf/pie is easy to remove from the tin once it's cooked. Be liberal with your greasing, and try to cut the paper as exactly as possible to keep the edges neat.

If I'm making fudge or something that doesn't need to be baked, I sometimes use foil as a liner as it's easier to squash into the corners. But if the recipe calls for greaseproof paper, wet your fingers and lightly dampen it to make it more pliable.

Melting chocolate

There are two methods: in a heat-proof bowl over a saucepan of boiling water, or in 20-second bursts in the microwave. Whichever one you choose, my advice is to do it slowly. Overheating chocolate will make it burn or 'seize', which is when it balls up into a solid mass and becomes useless. Try not to stir it, either: this can make the chocolate go grainy. Swirl the bowl instead.

Sugar temperatures

Sugar's a tricksy little ingredient, especially when it's being caramelized in a pan. You've got to get it to just the right stage so it doesn't crystallize or burn, and this means standing over the pan, waiting and watching it like a hawk. A sugar thermometer comes in handy, but if you don't have one you can measure it by time or colour. Each recipe that calls for sugar to be heated has detailed instructions on what to do – ignore them at your peril!

Brands

Nobody likes a name-dropper, and I've tried to avoid mentioning brands where possible. But if I say 'chocolate hazelnut spread' when everybody knows I mean Nutella, it can all get a bit silly. So please excuse the mention of Mars bars, Terry's Chocolate Orange, Oreo cookies and so on – and feel free to use alternative brands. They're just suggestions; you can use whichever variety you prefer.

AND FINALLY . . .

This whole book has been an exercise in experimentation. So my final word of advice before you begin is just that: experiment. If a recipe calls for a particular ingredient and you don't have any, improvise. If you don't like the flavour I've suggested but want to try baking something anyway, swap it. Some of the recipes have suggestions at the end for alternative bakes. But don't be afraid to mix things up a little – that's the whole idea.

KITCHEN TOOLS

Most of the ingredients in this book are store-cupboard basics – things I hope you'll have in your house, hiding away on the top shelf or forgotten at the back of the fridge.

But when it comes to equipment – and I'm talking baking trays, lolly moulds and crumble dishes – it's useful to know what you might need before you get halfway through a recipe and realize you don't have the right-sized tin. My top tip here is to read everything from start to finish – ingredients and method – before you start baking, so there aren't any surprises along the way.

There's nothing too niche in this list; they're everyday essentials that most bakers will have anyway. But if you're coming to this as a newbie and don't want to stock up on everything at once, I've put stars beside the absolute must-haves to help you decide.

You can pick most of them up for under a tenner at any cookware shop or at bigger supermarkets. And don't worry if yours are slightly different sizes to mine – a few centimetres here or there won't make a massive difference.

CAKE AND LOAF TINS

Non-stick, spring-form (this means you can push the bottom out) cake tins are best

- Small round cake tin: 20cm across *
- Medium round cake tin: 23cm across
- Standard loaf tin: 22cm x 12cm x 7cm *

BAKING TRAYS AND DISHES

Ceramic or aluminium, as long as they're non-stick

- Small baking tray: 25cm x 18cm x 5cm
- Square baking tray: 25cm x 25cm x 5cm *
- Large baking tray: 35cm x 24cm x 5cm
- Round pie dish: 20cm across
- Rectangular lasagne/crumble dish: 38cm x 25cm x 5cm *
- Deep pudding dish: capacity at least 2 litres
- Several large flat metal baking sheets *
- 12-hole muffin tray *

ELECTRICALS

None of these are essential, but they'll make your life an awful lot easier

- Blender or Magimix
- Electric whisk
- Electronic scales
- Slow cooker: capacity at least 3.5 litres

UTENSILS

- Spatula *
- Palette knife *
- Set of round and fluted cutters: 5cm and 7cm

- Pastry brush
- Sugar thermometer
- Ice cream scoop
- Piping bag and assorted nozzles

DÉCOR AND SERVING DISHES

- Large ceramic serving bowl
- Set of six matching ramekins, martini glasses, tumblers or serving bowls *
- Muffin cases *
- Petit-four cases
- Polystyrene/Paper cups
- Wooden lolly sticks and/or cake-pop sticks
- Wooden skewers *
- Cocktail sticks

MISCELLANEOUS BITS AND BOBS

- Mixing bowls, varying sizes *
- Heatproof jug
- Pizza stone
- Griddle pan
- Plastic lolly moulds – set of six and eight *
- Silicone cake-pop moulds
- Silicone ice-cube tray
- Lots and lots of airtight storage tins *
- Freezer-safe containers: capacity 500ml and 1 litre
- Aluminium foil
- Cling film
- Greaseproof paper or baking parchment: TONS of the stuff. I got through 34 10-metre rolls while writing this book *

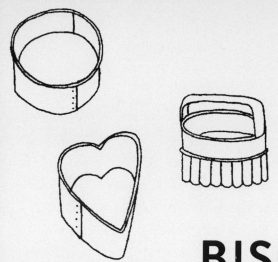

BISCUITS

Peanut butter cookies

Grandma's shortbread rounds

Hazelnut biscuits

Cocoa cookies

Pecan pie cookies

Cinnamon crispies

Fifteens

Chewy granola cookies

Flapjacks

Coconut macaroons

Banana bites

Giant caramel cookie

PEANUT BUTTER COOKIES

MAKES AROUND 25 COOKIES

These crispy little mouthfuls are the perfect dunkers for tea – or you can make like an American and have them with a glass of icy-cold milk. They're buttery and oh-so-nutty, but not too sweet.

260g crunchy peanut butter	200g caster sugar	1 egg

Preheat the oven to 195°C/175°C fan.

Put the ingredients in a large bowl and mix well until combined. It should all come together into a ball of dough. If the mixture is still quite gooey (this depends on the type and temperature of your peanut butter), use a pair of teaspoons to complete the next step.

Take chunks of the dough and roll them into balls the size of a 50p piece. Place these on a baking sheet lined with greaseproof paper, around 5cm apart. Use a fork to flatten each ball of dough to around 1cm thick.

Bake for approximately 20 minutes (a few minutes less if you prefer them squidgy).

Cool on a wire rack before serving.

 TIP: *If you don't have peanut butter to hand or want something that tastes a little less obviously nutty, try the cookies with almond or cashew butter instead. These won't be as strongly flavoured but will do the same job – buy the crunchy variety if you can get it.*

GRANDMA'S SHORTBREAD ROUNDS

MAKES 24 ROUNDS

My amazing grandma, who taught me to bake many years ago, used to make the world's best shortbread. Better still, it has only three ingredients in it. This is her recipe – light, buttery and melt-in-your-mouth delicious. It's an oldie but a goodie.

200g unsalted butter, softened	125g icing sugar, plus a little extra to sprinkle	225g plain flour, plus extra for dusting

5cm round cutter

Cream the butter and icing sugar together, covering the bowl with a tea towel to begin with so that the icing sugar doesn't fly everywhere. When fully combined, sift in the flour and mix to a soft dough.

Bring the dough together in your hands (don't worry if it's a little sticky at this stage) and place it in a bowl in the fridge for 20 minutes.

Take the dough out of the fridge, dust a clean, dry worktop and a rolling pin with some plain flour, and roll out the dough to a thickness of around 1cm. Using the round cutter (or the rim of a small glass or mug) cut circles out of the dough and place them on two baking sheets lined with greaseproof paper, around 3cm apart.

Prick each round a few times with a fork before putting the tray back in the fridge for another half-hour. When the time's nearly up, preheat the oven to 170°C/150°C fan. Bake the rounds for 35 minutes, switching the trays halfway through.

Take the rounds out when they're a pale golden colour – too long and they'll go crispy. Allow them to cool on a wire rack before dusting with icing sugar.

HAZELNUT BISCUITS

MAKES AROUND 20 BISCUITS

The Italians call these little gems 'brutti ma buoni', which means 'ugly but good'. They're definitely not going to win any beauty contests, but the combination of fluffy egg whites and toasted nuts is a winner. Try them on the side of a steaming cappuccino.

200g whole hazelnuts, skin on	3 egg whites	175g caster sugar

Preheat the oven to 195°C/175°C fan.

Tip the hazelnuts on to a baking sheet and roast for 12 to 15 minutes, or until they're toasty brown. Allow the nuts to cool, then tip them into a food processor. Blitz until they resemble breadcrumbs.

In a separate bowl, whisk the egg whites to stiff peaks, then slowly stir in the sugar, a spoonful at a time, followed by the ground nuts. You should end up with a thick, crumbly paste.

Arrange heaped teaspoons of the mixture on two baking sheets lined with greaseproof paper, leaving around 3cm between.

Bake for 25 minutes or until just crisp, switching the trays halfway through. The biscuits should still be slightly soft inside – too well done and you risk breaking your teeth!

COCOA COOKIES

MAKES 16 COOKIES

Bittersweet lumps of goodness, these cookies really hit the spot when you're craving something sweet. They're vegan and free from added sugar, too, so you don't need to feel guilty.

2 ripe bananas, peeled	80g cocoa powder	120g crunchy almond butter (or any other nut butter)

Mash the bananas in a bowl using a fork. Measure out the cocoa powder and almond butter into a separate bowl, and mix together. Add the bananas to the cocoa and almond mixture, a spoonful at a time, and gradually blend the whole lot into a thick dough.

Lay a sheet of cling film on a flat surface and place the dough on top. Wrap it up inside the cling film and roll to make a long cylinder, around 5cm in diameter. Place the wrapped cylinder flat in the freezer for 25 minutes, to harden.

At this stage, preheat the oven to 200°C/180°C fan.

Take the cylinder of dough out of the freezer, remove the cling film, and use a serrated knife to slice it into 1cm discs.

Space the cookies out on a baking sheet lined with greaseproof paper, and bake for around 20 minutes or until they begin to crisp up.

Transfer to a wire rack and allow to cool completely before eating. The cookies will harden as they cool, but the finished texture should be somewhere between a biscuit and a brownie.

 TIP: *Dust the cookies with icing sugar to make them look smarter and taste sweeter.*

PECAN PIE
COOKIES

150g pecan halves

+

150g pitted dates
(I use Medjool –
they're the plumpest,
juiciest kind)

+

3 tablespoons
maple syrup

PECAN PIE COOKIES

MAKES 12–14 COOKIES

These sweet, nutty cookies remind me of pecan pie. They're cooked at such a low heat they're more dehydrated than baked, but this gives them a delicious, toffee-like chewy texture.

150g pecan halves	150g pitted dates (I use Medjool – they're the plumpest, juiciest kind)	3 tablespoons maple syrup

Preheat the oven to 170°C/150°C fan.

Hold back 12 pecan halves and put the remainder in a blender. Blitz to tiny pieces.

Do the same with all the dates. (Be careful, though, as they'll stick to the blade and can clog up the blender. If you're worried about this, you can also chop them finely by hand.)

Mix the nuts and dates together until combined, then stir in the maple syrup. Use teaspoons to pick up small heaps of the mixture and place them on a baking sheet lined with greaseproof paper, a few centimetres apart. Use the back of one spoon or a fork to flatten them down. Place a pecan half on top of each.

Bake for around 45 minutes, or until the cookies are just holding together, then let them cool completely on the baking sheet.

 TIP: *You can leave these cookies raw if you prefer, but you'll need to give them 2 to 3 hours in the coldest part of the fridge to set first – and keep them in there to stop them from melting.*

CINNAMON CRISPIES

MAKES AROUND 16 CRISPIES

Some people think cinnamon is just for Christmas, but I couldn't disagree more. These crispy little biscuits are buzzing with the stuff, making them spicy and scrumptious – and they don't contain any sugar, so you can eat them whenever you like.

2 ripe bananas, peeled	3 teaspoons ground cinnamon	80g desiccated coconut

Preheat the oven to 200°C/180°C fan.

Gently mash the bananas in a bowl with a fork, then put them in a food processor along with the cinnamon. Blitz for 5 minutes, until the mixture comes together and is nice and fragrant.

Add half the coconut, blitz, then add the rest. Continue to mix until fully blended. The biscuit dough should be reasonably stiff but still moist.

Use a pair of teaspoons to drop small blobs of the dough on to a baking sheet lined with greaseproof paper, around 2cm apart. Round off the edges and press them down using a fork, making a criss-cross pattern on the top of each.

Bake for 20 to 25 minutes, until golden brown, rotating the tray halfway through. The crispies are yummiest eaten still warm, straight out of the oven.

CHEWY GRANOLA COOKIES

MAKES 10 MEDIUM-SIZED COOKIES

These are my throw-together-whatever-you-can-find-in-the-cupboard cookies: oaty granola, a half-tub of Biscoff biscuit spread and a couple of eggs. They're chewy in the middle, crisp on the outside and tastier than anything you can buy in the shops.

225g granola, flavour of your choice	200g Biscoff biscuit spread (if you can't find this, use peanut butter, smooth or crunchy, or chocolate hazelnut spread)	2 eggs

Preheat the oven to 180°C/160°C fan.

Pour the granola into a large bowl. In a separate bowl, mix the spread with the eggs until combined (if you try to do this all in one bowl, you'll get granola flying everywhere). Pour the egg mixture over the granola and stir well to combine.

Use a pair of teaspoons to place dollops of the mixture on two baking sheets lined with greaseproof paper, spaced a good 2–3cm apart. My cookies are around 1cm thick and 8cm wide, but you can make them as big or small as you want. Use a fork to press down the tops and neaten the sides.

Bake for 25 to 30 minutes or until just starting to brown on top. Switch the trays halfway through to make sure all the cookies are evenly baked.

Give them 5 minutes to cool on the baking sheets, then transfer to a wire rack. The cookies will keep for 3 to 4 days in an airtight container.

FLAPJACKS

MAKES 24 FLAPJACKS

I've tried so many flapjack recipes over the years, but always come back to the good old traditional one. There are no frills – just oats, syrup and butter – but they're hard to beat. I make mine in the bottom of a cake tin and slice them into chunky, chewy triangles.

200g unsalted butter	300g golden syrup	350g rolled oats (not jumbo oats – the little ones stick together better)

2 small round cake tins (20cm across)

Preheat the oven to 180°C/160°C fan, and butter and line the cake tins.

Melt the butter with the syrup in a saucepan over a medium heat, removing from the hob before the mixture starts to bubble. Pour over the oats in a large bowl, and mix thoroughly.

Press the mixture down into the cake tins using the back of a spoon so it is tightly packed and the top is flat and even.

Bake for approximately 30 minutes, until golden on top. Keep an eye on the flapjacks as they bake – remember, all ovens are different.

While they're still hot, use a sharp knife to score the flapjacks in each tin into twelve triangular pieces, taking care not to let too many oats come loose. Allow them to cool completely in the tins before removing. This is a bit fiddly, so take your time. They should be toffee-like on top but still crumbly in the middle.

 TIP: *For a healthier, dairy-free alternative, you can use coconut oil – the same weight when melted – instead of butter.*

FIFTEENS

MAKES 10–12 SLICES

Fifteens are a Northern Irish delicacy, so called because they contain fifteen of everything. I grew up eating them by the dozen. The originals contain glacé cherries and coconut, but I've given mine a twist by using caramel digestives. Once you've tasted them, you'll see what all the fuss is about …

1 x 300g packet of caramel digestives (you can use plain or chocolate if you prefer)	300g condensed milk (around ¾ of a tin)	15 marshmallows

Put 15 digestives in a ziplock bag, squeeze all the air out and bash with a rolling pin until they're crushed into crumbs. Tip the digestives into a bowl and add the condensed milk.

Chop the marshmallows into quarters (I find scissors work better than a knife, as it's very sticky work) and add to the biscuit mix. Stir until it's all combined.

Lay a large rectangle of cling film (at least 50cm long) on a flat surface. Put the remaining digestives from the packet into the ziplock bag and crush as before. Scatter them over the cling film so they cover the central area.

Spoon the mixture from the bowl on to the cling film, on top of the crushed digestives. Take the top and bottom of the cling film and fold them together over the top of the mixture. Twist the two ends like a cracker, compressing the mixture inside.

Fold the ends into the centre and roll the biscuit mixture a few times on the table to neaten it. You're aiming for a nice fat log, around 10cm in diameter. Put it on a plate or baking tray and place in the fridge to harden overnight. When it's ready, slice the log into 1cm-thick slices – and dig in!

 TIP: *You don't need to store the fifteens in the fridge after they've set; an airtight tin will do fine.*

COCONUT MACAROONS

MAKES 14 LARGE MACAROONS

Crisp and golden on the outside, slightly chewy in the centre – there's a knack to getting these little beauties right. But I guarantee there'll be no complaints if you have to try them again and again, just to be completely sure…

3 egg whites	115g icing sugar	250g desiccated coconut
	Ice cream scoop	

Preheat the oven to 190°C/170°C fan.

In a large bowl, whisk the egg whites with the icing sugar for around 8 minutes until very pale and thick. The consistency should be slightly gloopier than double cream. (If you have an electric or stand mixer, use this rather than a hand whisk – it'll make the job a lot easier, and less messy.)

Stir in the desiccated coconut, and mix thoroughly. Test the consistency of the macaroon mix by picking up a teaspoonful and rolling it into a ball in your hands. These quantities should work, but whisking egg whites is a very imprecise science and you want to get it right.

If it's too dry, add one more egg white. If it's too wet, add more coconut. Do this a little at a time and mix between each addition. Once it all sticks together, it's ready to go.

Use the ice cream scoop (or a pair of dessert spoons) to pick up blobs of macaroon mix and drop them on to a baking sheet lined with greaseproof paper, around 3cm apart.

Bake for around 25 minutes, or until the tops are just starting to brown. You may need to rotate the tray halfway through cooking to even out the heat.

Transfer to a cooling rack to crisp up, then serve.

BANANA BITES

MAKES AROUND 26 BITES

Half banana bread, half flapjack, these bites are just the right mix of healthy and comfortingly squidgy. You can swap the raisins for all sorts of sweeter alternatives, from cranberries and chopped nuts to chocolate-dipped raisins and Smarties – or just throw the lot in.

3 ripe bananas, peeled	200g rolled oats	150g raisins

Preheat the oven to 200°C/180°C fan.

Mash the bananas in a bowl using a fork until they form a gooey, thick liquid. Stir in the rolled oats and the raisins, mixing thoroughly so the raisins are distributed evenly throughout.

Arrange heaped teaspoonfuls of the mixture in rows around 2cm apart, on a baking sheet lined with greaseproof paper. (You may need a second baking sheet, depending on how big yours is.)

Bake for approximately 20 minutes, until just turning golden brown. If you've used two baking sheets, swap them in the oven halfway through so they cook evenly.

Allow the bites to cool on the baking sheet before prising them off (they can be very sticky). Put each one into a paper petit-four case before serving.

 **TIP:** *The bites should keep for several days in a tin.*

GIANT CARAMEL COOKIE

SERVES 6 ... OR ONE VERY HUNGRY PERSON

This tasty little number should technically be in the cake section – but I find it much more decadent to think of it as a giant biscuit. It's crumbly, cakey and will make you feel like a big kid. You can munch it whole or slice it into wedges like a pie.

115g salted butter, softened	6 tablespoons golden syrup	170g self-raising flour

Round pie dish (20cm across)

Preheat the oven to 200°C/180°C fan and grease the pie dish.

Cream the butter and 5 tablespoons of the syrup together in a bowl until the mixture turns pale and fluffy. Sift in the flour, and mix well.

Put the cookie dough into the pie dish, and use the back of the wooden spoon to spread it out to the edge. Drizzle the remaining tablespoon of golden syrup over the top.

Bake for 25 minutes until golden brown. Don't worry if it sinks a little when it comes out of the oven – this will just add to the chewy, caramelly texture. The baked syrup on top should give the surface a slight crunch, but underneath it'll still be soft.

Allow the cookie to cool completely in the dish before sliding it out (a fish slice or palette knife can come in handy here) and slicing it up like a pie.

CAKES

Christmas cake

Gooey chocolate orange cake

Sticky pineapple slice

Log cake

Honey cake

Slow and steady banana bread

Apple sandwich

Ice cream bread

Flourless walnut cake

Madeira sponge

Peanut butter mug cake

Ginger lemon freezer cake

CHRISTMAS CAKE

SERVES 12

Rich, spiced and packed full of juicy raisins, cherries and peel, it's hard to beat a proper fruit cake at Christmas. My take on this festive classic is super-simple, using chocolate-flavoured milk to create that heady sponge, laden with plump, bursting fruits.

530g mixed dried fruit (I use one containing peel, glacé cherries, sultanas, raisins and cranberries)	500ml chocolate milk	175g self-raising flour

Medium round cake tin (23cm across)

Start preparing this cake at least 12 hours before you want to eat it.

Put the dried fruit and chocolate milk in a bowl, cover in cling film and leave them for as long as possible so the fruits absorb the liquid and become plump and juicy. You'll know it's ready when the milk thickens and the fruit swells to the top of the liquid.

Preheat the oven to 180°C/160°C fan, and grease and line the cake tin.

When the fruit is ready, sift in the flour and stir until fully combined. Pour into the tin, bang it on a table a couple of times to get rid of any air bubbles, and smooth out the top using a palette knife.

Bake for around 2 hours, or until a skewer inserted into the middle comes out clean. Allow to cool in the tin before turning out on to a wire rack. This won't keep as long as traditional Christmas cake, but it will last a couple of weeks in a sealed tin. It tastes great with a dollop of brandy cream.

 TIP: *Try other flavours of milk (such as coffee or banana), or orange juice to give a lighter sponge. And if you miss that layer of white fondant on top, sift icing sugar over some Christmassy stencils – stars, snowflakes or trees – for a snowy finish.*

GOOEY CHOCOLATE ORANGE CAKE

3 x 175g Terry's
Chocolate Oranges

+

110g unsalted butter

+

8 eggs

GOOEY CHOCOLATE ORANGE CAKE

SERVES 8–10 (GENEROUS SLICES)

This gooey cake reminds me of the Bruce Bogtrotter scene in Roald Dahl's Matilda – it's so deliciously dense and chocolaty. The orange flavour makes it warming and citrussy, while the lack of flour makes it super-squidgy inside – a bit like a mousse.

3 x 175g Terry's Chocolate Oranges	110g unsalted butter	8 eggs

Medium round cake tin (23cm across)

Preheat the oven to 195°C/175°C fan, and grease and line the cake tin.

Put 450g chocolate orange and all the butter in a small heatproof bowl suspended over a saucepan of boiling water, and heat gently until they melt, or microwave them in 20-second bursts until they've completely melted. Mix sparingly – you don't want the chocolate to go grainy.

Meanwhile, break the eggs into a large bowl and whisk until pale and fluffy. Do this for longer than you think you should – when you're just about ready to stop, give it another 30 seconds. All the air in the cake comes from the eggs, so give them a good 5 minutes with an electric whisk (double this time if you're doing it by hand).

Take the chocolate and butter mixture off the heat, and allow to cool slightly. Transfer the mixture to a large bowl and slowly add the whisked egg, one spoonful at a time, folding it in gently. Continue until you've added all the egg and it's completely combined.

Pour the cake mix into the tin and bake for 40 to 45 minutes, or until the top is just set. Don't over-bake – you want it to stay nice and squidgy inside.

Allow the cake to cool completely in the tin before serving. Use the remaining segments of chocolate orange to decorate it, or melt them and drizzle over the top.

The cake tastes best slightly chilled – when the goo sets to a wobbly mousse – and it'll keep in the fridge for up to 5 days.

STICKY PINEAPPLE SLICE

SERVES 10

There's a scene in the 1989 film Steel Magnolias *where Truvy (played by Dolly Parton) reels off her recipe for 'Cuppa Cuppa Cuppa' cake. It's more a crispy cobbler than a cake, but it's ridiculously easy to throw together and looks impressive. This is my version.*

150g self-raising flour	200g caster sugar	1 x 432g tin of pineapple in syrup or juice

Standard loaf tin (22cm x 12cm x 7cm) – or, if you don't have one, you can bake it for the same amount of time in a small round cake tin (20cm across)

Preheat the oven to 200°C/180°C fan, and grease and line the loaf tin.

Sift the flour into a mixing bowl, and add the sugar.

Hold back one ring or a couple of chunks of pineapple from the tin then, in a separate bowl, mash the remaining pineapple in its syrup or juice and add this to the flour and sugar mixture. Use a blender if you need one – I like to do mine with a fork so there are still a few chunks left. Mix well until all the ingredients are combined.

Pour the mixture into the loaf tin (don't worry – it's supposed to be very liquid in texture), and bake for 60 minutes. You'll know it's ready when it's golden brown on top or a skewer inserted into the middle of the cake comes out clean.

Turn out on to a wire cooling rack. Before serving, decorate the loaf with the leftover pineapple.

 TIP: *Try using different tinned fruit – peaches or pears – for an alternative flavour.*

LOG CAKE

SLICES INTO 8–10 PIECES

Laden with butter and sugar, this decadent cake isn't one for every day – but it'll do nicely for a special occasion or a wet Sunday afternoon. It'll keep in the fridge for a week, or you can slice it and store it in pieces in a tin for 3 to 4 days.

100g unsalted butter	200g dark chocolate	16 plain digestive biscuits (around 250g)

Standard loaf tin (22cm x 12cm x 7cm)

Grease and line the loaf tin.

Put the butter and chocolate in a large heatproof bowl, and microwave them in 20-second bursts until they've completely melted, or in a small heatproof bowl suspended over a saucepan of boiling water. Mix together using a wooden spoon.

Put half the digestives in a small plastic bag, seal it and bash them with a rolling pin until they turn into crumbs. Add the biscuit crumbs to the chocolate and butter, and mix thoroughly.

Crumble the other half of the biscuits into the mixture, keeping the chunks nice and big. Give everything a quick mix so it all comes together, then transfer to the loaf tin. Use a spoon to pack it tightly into the tin, squeezing it into all the corners, and level out the top.

Put the cake in the fridge for an hour to set, then turn it out on to a board and slice it into thick pieces to serve.

 TIP: *You can use Hobnobs instead of digestive biscuits, or melt fruit and nut, milk or white chocolate instead of plain.*

HONEY CAKE

SERVES 8-10

This simple, one-layer cake is dense, moist and syrupy. It uses almonds instead of flour, which gives it a rich, toasty texture, and whisked egg whites to give it height.

4 eggs	5 tablespoons runny honey	150g flaked almonds

Small round cake tin (20cm across)

Preheat the oven to 190°C/170°C fan, and grease and line the cake tin.

Separate the eggs, and whisk the whites to stiff peaks. Beat the yolks with 4 tablespoons of the honey, mixing well.

Blitz 125g of the flaked almonds in a food processor to grind them. Put the remaining 25g on a baking sheet and, as the oven gets hot, pop them in for 5 to 10 minutes to toast them. Keep an eye on them; they'll colour very quickly.

Mix the ground almonds with the egg yolks and honey, and gradually fold in the egg whites using a metal spoon, being careful not to over-mix and beat out all the air.

Transfer the mixture to the cake tin and bake for 25 minutes, lowering the temperature for the final 10 minutes to 180°C/160°C fan.

Allow the cake to cool completely in the tin before turning it out on to a wire rack. Drizzle the final tablespoon of honey over the top, before sprinkling over the toasted almonds.

The cake will keep for 1 to 2 days in an airtight tin – if it lasts that long …

SLOW AND STEADY BANANA BREAD

SERVES 8-10

You can't beat good old banana bread – except with one that's made in a slow cooker, making it even more indulgent and comforting than the original. You'll need a large, oval slow cooker for this (mine is a 3.5-litre Crock-Pot), just big enough to fit a loaf tin inside.

3 ripe bananas, peeled	280g self-raising flour	1 x 397g tin of sweetened condensed milk

Standard loaf tin (22cm x 12cm x 7cm)
Large slow cooker (capacity at least 3.5 litres)

Pour a cup of cold water into the slow cooker and set it to high, then grease and line the loaf tin. While the slow cooker heats up, mash the bananas in a bowl using a fork.

In another bowl, sift the flour and slowly fold in the mashed bananas, still using the fork so as not to punch all the air out of the mixture. Once it's all combined, pour in the condensed milk, using a spatula to scrape out the inside of the tin.

When the batter is just combined, pour it into the loaf tin. Place the tin inside the slow cooker (don't worry if it doesn't quite touch the bottom) and cover it with a sheet of greaseproof paper. Put the slow cooker lid on top to seal the bread inside. This way, it steams rather than bakes – and you'll get a dense, squidgy texture.

Leave for around 2 hours and 30 minutes, or until the loaf has stopped rising but still has a slight wobble. I check mine after 2 hours and then every 10 minutes, just to be sure. Remove from the slow cooker, take the greaseproof paper off the top and blast it in a hot (240°C/220°C fan) oven for 10 to 15 minutes to give a crispy coating. Allow to cool in the tin, then slice generously.

APPLE SANDWICH

SERVES 10–12

My mum came up with this teatime treat by accident, when she swapped wholemeal flour for self-raising – and ended up with a light, feathery sponge, sandwiched together with gooey apple sauce. The sweetness all comes from the fruit, so it's not laden with sugar.

150g self-raising flour	4 eggs	250g apple sauce

2 small round cake tins (20cm across)

Preheat the oven to 200°C/180°C fan, and grease and line the cake tins.

Sift the flour. Separate the eggs into two large bowls, putting the yolks in a larger one. Whisk the egg whites until stiff, using an electric whisk if possible.

Beat the egg yolks with a wooden spoon, and add 150g of the apple sauce. Beat the yolks and sauce together for at least 2 minutes, until the mixture turns pale yellow and all the lumps disappear.

Using a metal spoon, fold the flour in carefully, followed by the egg whites. Split the mixture between the two tins and put them into the oven quickly (don't leave them sitting around too long, or the air will start to drop out).

Bake for approximately 15 minutes, or until the top turns a pale golden colour. Remove from the oven, allow to cool slightly, then turn them out on to a cooling rack.

When cold, sandwich the cakes together with the remainder of the apple sauce, spreading it evenly over the top of one with a palette knife.

Slice and serve – preferably with a large pot of tea.

ICE CREAM BREAD

300g good-quality
vanilla ice cream

+

225g
self-raising flour

+

2 tablespoons
multicoloured
sprinkles

ICE CREAM BREAD

SLICES INTO 8–10 PIECES

This simple, sweet, cakey bread, made from melted ice cream, is great fun for kids of any age – including grown-up ones! It reminds me of one of Willy Wonka's mad creations, and it certainly looks a bit bonkers, but the taste is great.

300g good-quality vanilla ice cream	225g self-raising flour	2 tablespoons multicoloured sprinkles

Standard loaf tin (22cm x 12cm x 7cm)

Preheat the oven to 205°C/185°C fan, and grease and line the loaf tin.

Weigh the ice cream out into a heatproof bowl and blast it for 10-second bursts in the microwave to melt it. You don't want it to get hot, just melted, so do it in stages.

Use an electric whisk to beat the ice cream until it is fluffy. Sift in the flour and stir briskly through so as not to lose all the air. Make sure the mixture is at room temperature – not hotter – before stirring in the sprinkles. If you do it while it's hot, they'll melt into the mixture and lose all their colour.

Pour the batter into the loaf tin, using a spatula to get it all out of the bowl. You can add some extra sprinkles on top if you want. Bake for 30 minutes, until golden brown on top.

Leave the bread in the tin for 5 minutes before turning it out on to a wire rack to cool. Slice and enjoy spread with lashings of salty butter.

 TIP: *This is a fun bread to experiment with – try chocolate chips instead of sprinkles, or different flavours of ice cream. Coffee is great, as are chocolate and honeycomb.*

FLOURLESS WALNUT CAKE

This light-as-a-feather sponge uses ground walnuts instead of flour, and super-fine icing sugar instead of caster, so the end result is like biting into a cloud. The trick is in the mixing – be gentle and take your time to get it just right.

250g whole walnuts	6 eggs	250g icing sugar, plus extra to decorate

Medium round cake tin (23cm across)

Preheat the oven to 210°C/190°C fan, and grease and line the cake tin.

Separate out 30g walnuts and set to one side. Put the rest into a blender and blitz into fine crumbs.

Separate the eggs into two bowls. Beat the icing sugar and the egg yolks together until light and fluffy. You might want to put a tea towel over the bowl to begin with – or the icing sugar will go everywhere. Start with a wooden spoon and, when the mixture turns pale, switch to a whisk. It should take 10 minutes in total by hand, or 3 to 4 minutes with an electric whisk. You'll know it's ready when it looks like thick cream. Once combined, stir the ground walnuts into this mixture.

In the other bowl, whisk the egg whites to soft peaks. You want them nice and airy – this is where the lightness of the sponge comes from. Use a metal spoon to fold the whites into the sugar and yolks mixture, a little at a time. It will start off quite thick – don't worry; as you add more whites it will combine more easily. Be gentle, and try not to over-mix.

Pour the batter into the lined tin. Bake for 35 minutes, or until a skewer inserted into the centre of the sponge comes out clean. It should still be nice and moist inside, with brown caramelized edges. Allow the cake to cool slightly before turning out on to a wire rack. Once cool, sift a dusting of icing sugar over the cake and top with the remaining walnuts, chopped, or whole if you prefer. Serve with freshly whipped cream.

MADEIRA SPONGE

SERVES 8

Madeira sponge is a British classic – slightly heavier and more moist than Victoria sponge, but with the same lovely vanilla flavour. This one is made with cornflour, which helps keep it light and fluffy with a golden crust on top.

4 eggs	140g caster sugar, plus a little extra for dusting	130g cornflour

Small round cake tin (20cm across)

Preheat the oven to 200°C/180°C fan, and grease and line the cake tin.

Crack the eggs into a bowl and whisk using an electric whisk for 3 to 4 minutes, until they double in size and turn a creamy yellow colour.

Add the sugar, and whisk again until combined. Don't be afraid to over-whisk at this stage – there's no raising agent so all the air needs to be beaten into the eggs. Sift in the cornflour (be careful – it's got the same consistency as icing sugar and can be a bit messy) and give it a quick stir to roughly combine. Then, whisk the whole mixture for another couple of minutes until it's thick and smooth. Pour the mixture into the cake tin and give it a couple of sharp taps on a table to get rid of any air bubbles. Bake for 25 minutes, or until a skewer inserted into the centre of the cake comes out clean.

Cool in the tin over a wire rack; don't worry if the cake sinks a little. Use a knife around the edge of the tin to carefully ease the cake out once it's cool. When you're ready to serve, dust the cake with a little extra caster sugar. Top with fresh fruit, poached pears or maraschino cherries, if you like – or you can even slice it in half and sandwich it together with some jam and whipped cream.

 TIP: *As the cake cools, pierce several holes in the top using a skewer. Instead of sprinkling the remaining sugar over the cake, mix it in a ramekin with the juice of 1 lemon, then pour this over the cake for an easy-peasy lemon drizzle.*

PEANUT BUTTER MUG CAKE

SERVES 1

Mug cakes are ideal if you don't have time to whip up a proper cake – and you can normally make them from a few odds and ends in the back of the cupboard. For me they bring back the magic of baking: put everything in a mug, give it a stir – and pop it in until it pings!

140g (roughly 3 tablespoons) crunchy peanut butter	30g granulated sugar	2 eggs

You'll need a suitable mug – a chunky ceramic one that can withstand the heat (you don't want a cracked cup) and that won't get too hot.
Look on the base for one that's microwave-proof.

Measure the peanut butter and sugar into the mug. Crack in the eggs, and whisk everything together using a fork. Once the batter is fully combined – it should go around three-quarters of the way up the mug – put it in the microwave and heat on high for 1 to 2 minutes.

In my 700W microwave (category D), it takes exactly 1 minute, 45 seconds – but don't worry if yours is different. Just watch through the glass so you can see the cake slowly rise around 2.5cm over the edge of the mug. It will sink a little as soon as the heat stops, but if it falls below the mug rim, blast it for another 5 to 10 seconds – it's ready when it stays risen.

Use an oven glove or tea towel on the handle of the mug to take it out of the microwave. Let the cake cool for a minute before digging in.

 TIP: *Try cashew or almond butter instead of peanut, or you can even use chocolate hazelnut spread. If you're feeling particularly indulgent, add another spoonful on top before eating – it will go all gooey as it starts to melt into the cake.*

GINGER LEMON
FREEZER CAKE

SERVES 8-10

This American dessert originated during World War One, when it was invented to use up odds and ends of stale cake and cold custard. Immersing biscuits in cream makes them turn soft and cake-like, so this has the consistency of a sponge laden with frozen, citrussy cream.

400ml whipping cream	280g ginger nut biscuits (roughly a whole packet)	3 heaped dessert spoons lemon curd

Medium round cake tin (23cm across)

Line the cake tin with cling film, making sure you not only wrap the base but cover the sides, leaving around a 2.5cm overhang to help you pull the cake out.

Whip the cream to soft peaks – this should take 3 minutes with an electric whisk. Add two dessert spoons of lemon curd and whisk to combine.

Now it's time to start filling the cake tin. Lay one layer of ginger biscuits over the bottom of the tin, starting with one in the centre and placing the others in a circle around it. You can break up biscuits to fill in the gaps if you wish, but I prefer to use eight ginger nuts per layer – one in the middle and a neat circle of seven surrounding it.

Spoon a third of the cream on top and spread it out so the biscuits are covered. Repeat with another two layers of biscuit and cream, making sure you leave some biscuits (there should be four if you're using a standard packet of ginger nuts) to crumble over the top.

Put the remaining dessert spoon of lemon curd in a small heatproof bowl and microwave for 10 to 15 seconds until it melts. Pour this over the top of the cake in a zigzag pattern.

Place the leftover biscuits in a ziplock bag, seal and bash with a rolling pin to turn them to chunky crumbs. Scatter these over the top of the melted curd.

Place the cake in the freezer for at least 4 hours or preferably overnight. Take it out 20 minutes before serving to allow it to soften and, if you like, top with a sprig of fresh mint.

TIP: *You can keep the cake in the freezer for up to 3 months.*

TRAYBAKES

Chocolate praline brownies

Apricot slice

Fruit puffs

Mini palmiers

Chocolate peanut squares

Snickers slice

Peanut butter cups

Popcorn clusters

Malteser traybake

Cornflake crunch

Ginger muffins

Nutty blondies

Healthy energy bars

Baklava

CHOCOLATE PRALINE BROWNIES

If you like Nutella, these are a must. They're rich, gooey and take just minutes to throw together. The key is in the cooking time – keep an eye on the mixture so it doesn't set too solid in the oven. You want them a little bit wobbly for maximum squidge.

65g self-raising flour	2 eggs	1 x 400g jar of Nutella (or any other brand of chocolate hazelnut spread)

Small baking tray (25cm x 18cm)

Preheat the oven to 200°C/180°C fan, and grease and line the baking tray.

Sift the flour into a mixing bowl, crack in the eggs and mix well with a wooden spoon. Scrape out the contents of a jar of Nutella and add this to the mixture, holding back 1 heaped tablespoon of the spread in a separate bowl. Stir everything together until the mixture is smooth.

Pour the mixture into the baking tray; spread it out with a spatula and bake for 25 minutes. You'll know they're ready when they're just set and starting to crack on top. Don't over-bake them as they will continue to cook in the tin and you want them to stay squidgy inside!

As the brownies cool, drizzle the remaining Nutella over the top to decorate. If it's too solid, microwave it for 10 seconds in a heatproof bowl first.

Slice into chunky squares or rectangles to serve.

 TIP: *I like to double the quantities in this recipe and make them in the same-sized tin for fat, squidgy brownies that are twice the height. They may need another 5 to 10 minutes in the oven to cook through.*

APRICOT SLICE

I love apricots – they're bursting with juice and sweetness – but they seem to have fallen out of favour in the baking world. This is my bid to bring them back to glory: a crumbly traybake made with fresh coconut oil and some crispy toasted almonds.

250g fresh (not dried) apricots	3 tablespoons coconut oil	100g flaked almonds

Small baking tray (25cm x 18cm)

Preheat the oven to 195°C/175°C fan, and line the baking tray with greaseproof paper.

I buy my apricots ready-chopped (lazy, I know), but if yours are bigger, spread them out on a chopping board and use a sharp knife to cut them into tiny pieces.

Transfer them to a food processer, add the coconut oil and blitz until the mixture is as close to purée as it will go. If your food processer is anything like mine, it won't go completely smooth – but lumps and bumps give the slice a nice texture.

Add three-quarters of the flaked almonds to the food processer, and pulse several times to combine.

Tip the mixture into the baking tray and use the back of a spoon to flatten it down and spread it out into all the corners. Scatter the remaining flaked almonds over the top.

Bake for 30 to 35 minutes, or until the almonds on top turn brown.

Leave to cool completely in the tin before cutting it into squares. This will keep for a week in an airtight tin.

FRUIT PUFFS

MAKES 10 PUFFS

These light, golden puffs make a nutritious breakfast or mid-morning snack. As they cook, the fruit juices will bubble and burst throughout the sponge, making them oh-so-moreish.

1 punnet of fresh blackberries (around 225g)	2 ripe bananas, peeled	4 eggs

12-hole muffin tray

Preheat the oven to 210°C/190°C fan.

Line the muffin tray with 10 paper cases. Place 3 or 4 blackberries in the bottom of each case.

Mash the bananas together. In a separate bowl, whisk the eggs, then add the mashed bananas. Using an electric whisk, beat the mixture thoroughly for several minutes until it is light and fluffy. This step is crucial if you want your muffins to be airy rather than flat and dense.

Divide the mixture between the muffin cases, filling each almost to the top.

Bake for around 15 to 20 minutes, or until risen and golden.

Allow to cool fully in the tin before eating – and eat them fast, as the fruit makes them very moist and they won't keep for more than a couple of days.

 TIP: *Why not try raspberries or blueberries instead of blackberries? Or, if you fancy something sweeter, put a teaspoonful of nut butter or chocolate spread in the bottom of each case.*

MINI PALMIERS

These crisp, light-as-a-pillow pastries are sheer heaven. I first tasted them in Madrid, where no bakery is ever without a stack of palmiers (from the French for 'palm tree') in the window. My mini ones are filled with cinnamon sugar, but you can also make them savoury.

1 x 215g ready-rolled frozen puff pastry	50g golden caster sugar	2 teaspoons ground cinnamon

Leave the pastry out of the freezer for several hours so it is soft and pliable.

Unroll one roll (packs generally contain two) on its paper and flatten it slightly with a rolling pin so it is a neat rectangle.

In a bowl, mix the sugar and cinnamon together. Sprinkle the cinnamon sugar evenly across the pastry so it coats the surface.

Starting on one of the two longer sides, and using the paper for grip, slowly roll the edge in towards the centre of the pastry rectangle, stopping when you get to the middle. Do the same on the other side, so the two rolls meet in the middle. The resulting shape should look like half a butterfly's wing.

Wrap the whole roll gently in the paper and place flat in the freezer for at least 30 minutes. This will help the palmiers hold their shape. Preheat the oven to 240°C/220°C fan.

Remove the pastry from the freezer and, using a sharp knife, slice the roll into 1cm slices. If the knife sticks, dampen it under the tap to make the cut cleaner.

Arrange the palmiers flat on baking sheets lined with greaseproof paper, around 5cm apart. You will probably need two, as the pastries expand during baking.

Bake for 15 to 20 minutes, or until the pastry is flaky and golden. Cool on a wire rack. Sprinkle any leftover cinnamon sugar over the top and eat them hot.

TIP: *Try making savoury palmiers filled with tapenade and sundried tomatoes or chopped herbs and soft cream cheese – around 50g of either filling.*

CHOCOLATE PEANUT SQUARES

MAKES 25 SQUARES

A sweet treat that's not bad for you? These chocolate nutty squares taste so good they should probably be illegal – but I won't tell anyone if you don't.

125g dark chocolate (over 70 per cent cocoa if possible)	200g unsalted roasted peanuts	200g pitted dates

Square baking tray (25cm x 25cm)

Chop the chocolate into small pieces using a sharp knife. Put the peanuts and dates in a food processor, and pulse until the mixture is crumbly. Add 40g of the chopped chocolate to the food processor, and pulse a little more to combine.

Line the baking tray with greaseproof paper, tip the mixture in and use a palette knife to spread it out and smooth the top.

Melt the remainder of the chocolate in a microwave or over a saucepan of boiling water, and pour it over the mixture in the tin. Gently warm a palette knife by dipping it into the pan of water or running it under water from the kettle or hot tap, and use this to smooth the top down.

Cover lightly with cling film and put the mixture in the fridge to harden. Once firm (it should take 2 to 3 hours), cut it into squares to serve.

SNICKERS SLICE

MAKES 18 PIECES

This indulgent traybake is so easy to make: just take your favourite chocolate bar, melt it in the microwave and add a few basic ingredients from the cupboard to turn it into a sponge. Whoever said baking was difficult?

8 x 48g Snickers bars	2 eggs	75g self-raising flour

Square baking tray (25cm x 25cm)

Preheat the oven to 195°C/175°C fan, and line the baking tray with greaseproof paper.

Break seven of the Snickers bars into a large heatproof bowl, and melt on high in the microwave. Stir every 20 seconds to stop them from burning.

Once the chocolate is fully melted, whisk thoroughly to get rid of as many lumps as you can (not including the peanuts). Add the eggs, sift in the flour and beat until fully combined.

Pour the batter into the prepared tin and bake for 30 minutes, or until spongy to the touch. Allow it to cool in the tin. Before slicing into squares, decorate with the remaining Snickers bar, chopped into chunks and scattered on top.

 TIP: *Experiment with flavours by using different chocolate bars, such as Mars or Boost. As long as they have a chocolate/caramel base, they'll work in exactly the same way.*

PEANUT BUTTER CUPS

MAKES 12 CUPS

Inspired by the American candies, these bite-sized salted peanut butter cups are a delicious afternoon pick-me-up. They're so simple to make, and great for a lunchbox treat.

400g milk chocolate	280g peanut butter	5g sea salt

12-hole muffin tray
Fine pastry brush or small (clean!) paintbrush

Line the muffin tray with paper or metallic cases.

Melt half the chocolate in a heatproof jug in the microwave (this makes it easy to pour), heating it in 20-second bursts so it doesn't burn, or in a heatproof bowl suspended over a saucepan of boiling water.

Pour the chocolate into the paper cases, dividing it evenly between them. Use the pastry brush or paintbrush to spread the chocolate around halfway up each paper case. Take your time – it can be fiddly to get a nice straight line. This creates the chocolate shell for the peanut butter to sit inside.

Place the muffin tray in the fridge for 30 minutes to allow the chocolate to set. Once set, put a heaped teaspoon of peanut butter into each chocolate mould, smoothing down the top with the back of a spoon.

Sprinkle half the salt over the peanut butter layer and place the tray in the freezer (so the peanut butter firms up) for around 15 minutes.

Melt the remaining chocolate and, once the peanut layer is hard, pour this over each cup, smoothing it out on top. Sprinkle over the remaining salt.

Place the tray back in the fridge for 2 hours to set.

Take the cups out of their cases and serve. They're best kept in the fridge so they don't melt, and they will stay fresh for a week.

POPCORN CLUSTERS

MAKES AROUND 25 CLUSTERS

Salty, sweet and light as a cloud, these little pink and white clusters will quickly become a family favourite. Serve them in bowls at parties or wrap them up and bring them to work or school for a burst of energy mid-afternoon.

100g mixed marshmallows (pink and white – use more pink if you want them rosy-coloured)	50g unsalted butter	100g salted popcorn

Line two baking sheets (or chopping boards) with greaseproof paper.

Melt the marshmallows and butter in a saucepan, stirring constantly so the mixture doesn't stick.

Tip the popcorn into a large bowl and pour the marshmallow mixture over the top. Use a wooden spoon to coat the popcorn. If you can't get it all out of the pan – it can be pretty sticky – put some popcorn back into the pan and swirl it around to soak it up.

Allow the mixture to cool slightly. At this stage, you might also want to soak the saucepan, as the marshmallow is really hard to get off once it's solidified.

Wet your hands and roll up your sleeves. Take palm-sized blobs of the popcorn mixture and roll them into balls. Space them out on the greaseproof paper to harden and let them set for around half an hour before tucking in.

MALTESER TRAYBAKE

Growing up, I can't remember a birthday party or school fair that didn't feature the iconic Malteser traybake. It's a hit with children, but the combination of crumbly honeycomb and sweet Milkybar chocolate is sure to tempt a few adult tastebuds, too.

300g white chocolate, such as Milkybar – buttons or bars will do	100g unsalted butter	200g Maltesers

Small baking tray (25cm x 18cm)

Grease and line the baking tray with greaseproof paper.

Melt the white chocolate in a heatproof bowl suspended over a saucepan of boiling water, or in the microwave in 20-second bursts, stirring only occasionally so it doesn't go grainy.

Add the butter and let this melt into the chocolate. Once the butter's in there, you'll need to stir it more regularly to stop it from curdling – so keep an eye on it.

While the mixture melts, put two-thirds of the Maltesers into a ziplock bag, seal it and bash with a rolling pin to crush them. Tip them into a big bowl.

Allow the melted butter and chocolate to cool slightly before pouring the mixture over the crushed Maltesers. The mixture will start turning brown as the milk chocolate melts, so stir it quickly to keep the marbled effect.

Tip this into the baking tray, spreading it out into all the corners, and press the remaining whole Maltesers down into the top.

Refrigerate for 2 to 3 hours before slicing into small, super-sweet squares.

CORNFLAKE CRUNCH

These little squares of crunchy, caramelized cornflakes are incredibly moreish. They work well for a children's party – or you can smarten them up with a drizzle of dark chocolate.

175g caster sugar	300g cornflakes	1 x 397g tin of sweetened condensed milk

Large baking tray (32cm x 25cm)

Line the baking tray with greaseproof paper.

Put the sugar in a saucepan over a medium heat and heat slowly until it caramelizes. It should take 5 to 10 minutes. Don't stir the mixture – this can make it go grainy. Swirl the pan if you want to even out the heat.

While the sugar caramelizes, put the cornflakes into a large bowl and scrunch them between your fingers to crush them slightly.

When the sugar is ready, add the condensed milk to the pan. Don't worry if the sugar solidifies at this stage – adding something cold to the hot pan is likely to have this effect. Just keep the pan over the heat and stir constantly until the sugar has all dissolved. This can take a while – up to 15 minutes – but you'll know it's ready when the liquid thickens and turns golden brown.

Pour this mixture over the cornflakes, and mix using a wooden spoon. Tip it into the tin and press down into the corners, using a cold metal spoon to even out the top layer. Set aside to cool in the tin before cutting into squares.

 TIP: *You can use any crispy breakfast cereal in this recipe, so try swapping the cornflakes for Rice Krispies, Crunchy Nut Cornflakes, Shredded Wheat or even Weetabix. Start with the same quantity and add more as needed to get the consistency just right.*

GINGER MUFFINS

MAKES 10 MUFFINS

Ginger beer is my all-time favourite fizzy drink, so using it in baking is a no-brainer for me. These muffins are light and airy with a warming, gingery kick. Try to use the most intensely flavoured beer you can find – I like Old Jamaica – to give the best taste.

300g self-raising flour	150g golden caster sugar	1 x 330ml can of ginger beer

12-hole muffin tray

Preheat the oven to 200°C/180°C fan, and put paper muffin cases in ten holes of the tray.

Sift the flour into a bowl and stir in the sugar. There isn't a huge amount of sugar in these muffins as the ginger beer is so sweet – so don't worry if it all seems a bit floury.

Slowly pour the ginger beer into the flour and sugar mixture. Be careful, as it will fizz, but it should settle down and combine eventually. Beat thoroughly to get rid of all the lumps. The mixture should be smooth but not too thick, a bit like pancake batter. Pour it into the muffin cases, filling each around two-thirds full.

Bake for 30 minutes, or until the muffins are risen and starting to turn brown on top.

You can eat them hot – they're delicious with stewed apples or poached pears as a dessert – or cold as a snack. For an extra gingery kick, sprinkle some ground ginger on top or add a teaspoonful of ginger curd.

NUTTY BLONDIES

MAKES 16 BLONDIES

Fudgy, gooey and nutty, these blondies are the perfect alternative to brownies. If you're still a bit wary of using vegetables in baking, this is a good place to start. The sweet potato texture mimics the effect of eggs, sugar and flour – and it's a sneaky dose of your five-a-day.

350g sweet potato (peeled and diced, or ready-prepared)	4 tablespoons white hot chocolate powder	160g almond butter

Square baking tray (25cm x 25cm)

Preheat the oven to 200°C/180°C fan. Line the baking tray with greaseproof paper.

Put the sweet potato in a saucepan, cover with water and bring to the boil. Let it bubble away for 7 minutes, or until it has softened.

Drain and mash the sweet potato using a fork. Do this back in the saucepan over the heat so any excess water evaporates off.

In a separate bowl, combine the white hot chocolate powder and almond butter. Add the sweet potato a spoonful at a time, and mix thoroughly. Taste the blondie mix at this stage – it may need a little more chocolate powder if you have a sweet tooth.

Tip it into the baking tray, spread it out using a palette knife and bake for 30 minutes, or until the top is set and the edges are starting to brown.

Allow it to cool in the tin before slicing into squares. If you have any in the cupboard, drizzle a little melted white chocolate over the top of the blondie.

HEALTHY ENERGY BARS

These healthy bars make a great elevenses snack. You can use prunes or apricots instead of dates, but they need to be soaked in hot water beforehand to make them nice and soft.

200g dried mixed fruit (sultanas, raisins, currants or cranberries)	250g nuts (cashews, walnuts, Brazil nuts, pecans or a mixed selection)	150g pitted dates

Square baking tray (25cm x 25cm)

Put all the ingredients in a food processor. Pulse a few times to make into crumbs, then process for another minute or so until the ingredients start to come together into a ball.

Line the baking tray with greaseproof paper and transfer the mixture to the tray. Use a palette knife to spread it into the corners and flatten out the top.

Refrigerate for a couple of hours, then remove from the fridge and cut into bars or squares.

TIP: *These keep well in the fridge, or you can freeze a batch for up to 2 months.*

BAKLAVA

1 x 270g ready-rolled filo
pastry sheets

+

300g mixed nuts (make sure
they include pistachios – these
are pretty crucial in baklava)

+

6 tablespoons
runny honey

BAKLAVA

MAKES AROUND 20 PIECES

This Middle Eastern delicacy is packed full of crunchy nuts and drenched in sweet, nectar-like honey. My recipe is a pared-down version – you can always fancy it up by stirring mixed spices (nutmeg, cinnamon, ginger) into the nuts.

1 x 270g ready-rolled filo pastry sheets	300g mixed nuts (make sure they include pistachios – these are pretty crucial in baklava)	6 tablespoons runny honey

Square baking tray or dish (25cm x 25cm)

Preheat the oven to 160°C/140°C fan, and grease the baking tray or dish with a little butter or oil.

Use a sharp knife to cut the filo into sheets exactly the same size as the base of the dish. You'll need at least nine. Lay them flat on a table on top of one another, covered with a damp tea towel so they don't crisp up and dry out. Keep and re-freeze any offcuts.

Chop the nuts into coarse chunks.

Now it's time to assemble your baklava. Start with two sheets of filo, then scatter around a quarter of the nuts on top. Sprinkle a little cold water over the top to dampen the pastry and help it all stick together – I just stick my hand in a glass and shake it out over the top.

Repeat three times, giving you four identical layers, or keep going until all the nuts and pastry – except one sheet – are used up. Lay this final, single sheet over the top.

Before it goes in the oven, use a sharp knife to cut the baklava. I do mine in four long rows, then slice these diagonally to make diamonds. Make sure you cut right down to the base of the pastry – it's fiddly, so take your time to avoid tearing the super-thin filo.

Bake the baklava for 50 minutes. You'll know it's ready when the top layer is crisp and brown.

Meanwhile, make the sticky topping. Put the honey in a saucepan and heat it gently for 5 to 10 minutes, until it melts and thins out. When the baklava is baked, spoon or pour the honey over the top. Return it to the oven for 10 minutes.

Allow it to cool completely in the dish – this is when it goes nice and sticky, so be patient. Re-score the lines you made earlier to make the baklava easier to take out. The baklava pieces will keep for several days in an airtight tin or in the fridge.

 TIP: *For a more authentic taste, use a flavoured honey – you can buy cinnamon or lavender varieties in most supermarkets.*

SWEET TREATS

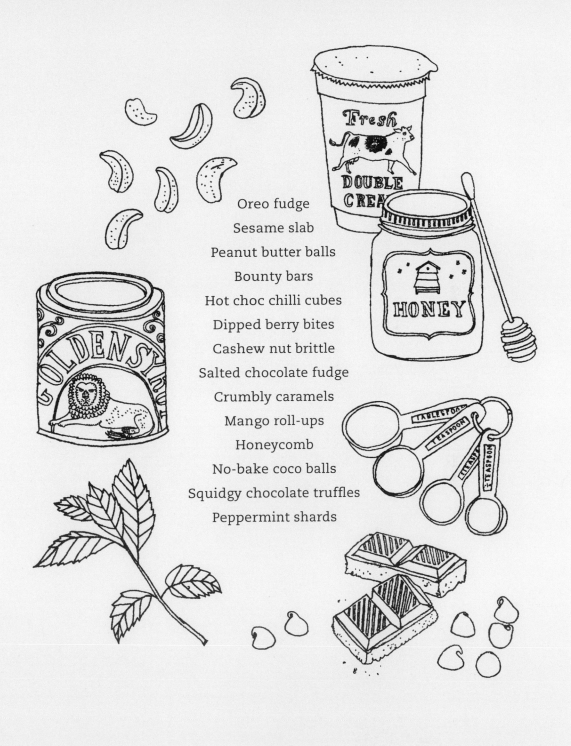

Oreo fudge
Sesame slab
Peanut butter balls
Bounty bars
Hot choc chilli cubes
Dipped berry bites
Cashew nut brittle
Salted chocolate fudge
Crumbly caramels
Mango roll-ups
Honeycomb
No-bake coco balls
Squidgy chocolate truffles
Peppermint shards

OREO FUDGE

MAKES AROUND 36 SQUARES

This is my go-to fudge recipe – but beware, you need a sweet tooth to truly appreciate it! It's delicious as a mid-afternoon treat or a mini indulgence after a meal.

400g white chocolate, chopped, or white chocolate chips	1 x 397g tin of sweetened condensed milk	14 Oreo cookies, crushed into small chunks

Square baking tray (25cm x 25cm)

Line the baking tray with aluminium foil, pressing it firmly into the corners and sides.

Put the white chocolate in a heatproof bowl and pour in the condensed milk. Microwave on full power for 30 seconds. Remove and stir, heating for 20-second bursts at a time, until all the chocolate has melted and the mixture is thick and smooth.

Spread half the crushed Oreos over the bottom of the tray. Allow the chocolate and condensed milk mixture to cool slightly before pouring it over the cookies, spreading it out evenly.

Arrange the remaining Oreos on top and press them down with your fingertips. Smooth the surface of the fudge using a knife dipped in boiling water so the top is flat.

Place the tray in the fridge for 4 to 5 hours to set. Use a sharp knife to cut the fudge into bite-sized pieces before serving.

 TIP: *If you don't have Oreo cookies, why not try this fudge with chocolate digestives, Hobnobs or bourbon biscuits? Anything chocolatey works a treat.*

SESAME SLAB

MAKES 18 SQUARES

This super-sweet, nutty slab is made from tahini, a Middle Eastern paste containing ground sesame seeds, which you can buy in large supermarkets or health-food shops. Rustle it up when you fancy a mouthful of something so sugary it makes your teeth ache.

150g granulated sugar	2 teaspoons coconut oil	100g tahini

Small baking tray (25cm x 18cm)
Optional: sugar thermometer

Line the baking tray with greaseproof paper, pressing it firmly into the corners to create a neat edge.

Heat the sugar in a saucepan over a medium heat until it caramelizes and turns amber. This should take around 6 minutes – or, if you're using a sugar thermometer, heat it to 118–120°C (this is known as 'firm ball' stage). Add the coconut oil, and mix it through.

Before decanting the tahini, use a clean spoon to give it a stir in the jar – it tends to separate, and you want the texture to be even throughout. Take the saucepan off the heat and add the tahini, stirring constantly. Work quickly, as the slab sets fast.

Use a spatula to scrape the mixture into the baking tray, and smooth out the top with a palette knife. Put it in the fridge to set for half an hour, before cutting into squares to serve.

Enjoy on the side of an espresso for a decadent after-dinner treat.

 TIP: *For an added crunch, sprinkle the slab with toasted coconut or sesame seeds.*

PEANUT BUTTER BALLS

MAKES 25-30 BALLS

My sister Anna introduced me to this healthy(ish) recipe, which is great for using up odds and ends from the cupboards. I'm a peanut butter fiend, so these are sheer bliss.

240g icing sugar	340g smooth peanut butter (an average-sized jar)	170g bitter dark chocolate, for dipping

Sift the icing sugar into a bowl and slowly add the peanut butter, combining each spoonful as you go. When the mixture has almost come together, use your hands to roll it into a ball. It should be the texture of crumbly pastry dough. Cover with cling film and put it in the fridge to chill for 30 minutes.

Separate the mixture into 50p-sized blobs. Roll into balls between your palms (slightly dampen your hands with some warm water if the mixture is crumbly). Place the balls on a plate covered with greaseproof paper, and chill them again for 30 minutes.

Meanwhile, melt the chocolate in a heatproof bowl over a saucepan of boiling water, or in a microwave in 20-second bursts, stirring in between so it doesn't burn. Once melted, allow the chocolate to cool slightly. Then dip the peanut butter balls one by one in the chocolate until each is fully covered, using a cocktail stick or fork to hold them if necessary.

Allow the excess chocolate to drip off, then place each ball on a wire rack over the plate. Leave in a cool place to harden, or pop them back in the fridge for half an hour before eating.

BOUNTY BARS

You can't beat a Bounty, and this homemade version is pretty special. The dark chocolate is chunky and bittersweet, while the gooey coconut filling is a tropical treat. This isn't one to make in a hot kitchen – the condensed milk can be messy to handle, so try to keep your cool.

200g desiccated coconut	1 x 397g tin of sweetened condensed milk	300g dark chocolate, for dipping

Mix the coconut and condensed milk together into a thick paste. Cover with cling film and chill in the fridge for 2 hours until it hardens into a pliable, solid mixture.

Dampen your palms with some warm water before flattening the coconut filling into a long, fat rectangle, around 1.3cm thick. Use a sharp knife to straighten up the edges, and slice it into bars. Spread the bars out on a plate covered in greaseproof paper and chill them in the fridge for another hour.

Meanwhile, melt 250g of the dark chocolate in a heatproof bowl over a saucepan of boiling water, or in a microwave in 20-second bursts, stirring in between so it doesn't burn. Allow it to cool slightly before tipping it on to a plate.

Remove the coconut bars from the fridge and dip them, one by one, in the chocolate. Use a spatula or the back of a teaspoon to make sure the top and four sides are covered (don't worry too much about the bottom). It's a messy process – I recommend keeping a bowl of warm water nearby to rinse your hands – and you'll need to work quickly so the filling doesn't soften.

Place the covered bars on a wire cooling rack, set this over the plate, and pop them back in the fridge for 10 minutes to set the chocolate. The rack allows any excess chocolate to drip off.

Melt the remaining 50g of chocolate and, when the bars are hard, drizzle this from side to side over the top of each one for a glossy, wavy topping. Allow them to set one last time – and enjoy!

HOT CHOC CHILLI CUBES

MAKES 18 CUBES

These fiery little cubes are made to be dunked in hot milk and stirred – giving you instant hot chocolate that's a million times better than anything that comes from a powder.

150g good-quality dark chocolate	1 tablespoon chilli oil	150ml double cream

Silicone ice-cube tray
Wooden lolly sticks

Wash and dry the ice-cube tray and prepare 18 wooden lolly sticks. It's important to use a silicone tray so you can push the moulds inside out to release the cubes. If you don't have one, you can try petit-four cases or cake-pop moulds for a different shape.

Chop the chocolate into small pieces, and mix with the chilli oil in a heatproof bowl.

Meanwhile, heat the cream in a heavy-bottomed saucepan for a few minutes, until it starts to bubble.

Remove the cream from the heat and pour it over the chocolate mixture. Whisk vigorously until all the chocolate has melted and the oil and cream are fully combined.

Use a jug or ladle to fill the ice-cube moulds with the hot chocolate mixture, being careful not to drip it over the rest of the tray. If you have any left over, put it into a small bowl – you can roll it into balls to make choc chilli bites later.

Refrigerate the cubes for an hour until they start to set. This is the time to insert the lolly sticks – you don't want to wait until they're too solid. Place one into the centre of each cube.

Put them in the freezer for 2 hours to set. Keep the cubes in the fridge or freezer (still in their tray) between uses to stop them from melting.

To make the perfect hot chocolate, heat some full-fat milk in a saucepan, stirring with a whisk to make it light and frothy. Tip it into your desired mug and serve with a hot choc chilli cube on the side. A few stirs and the cube should dissolve into the milk.

Sit back, put your feet up – and enjoy your chocolaty drink with a kick.

20g
freeze-dried
raspberries

170g white almond
butter (this is the one
without the skins, so
it's paler in colour –
if you can't find it,
normal almond butter
is fine)

100g white chocolate

DIPPED BERRY BITES

MAKES AROUND 14 BITES

Freeze-dried fruits are a baker's dream: little explosions of flavour that burst with sweetness. You can find them in the baking aisle of most supermarkets – they're not cheap, but you don't need much. These bites combine freeze-dried raspberries with marzipan-y almond butter.

Put the freeze-dried raspberries in a blender and blitz them to a fine powder. Keep your face away from the blender when you take off the lid: the berry dust can make you cough.

Stir the raspberries into the almond butter until fully combined. Run a dessert spoon coated in almond butter around the inside of your mixer if you can't get all the dust out – it'll pick it up like a vacuum cleaner.

Roll small balls of the mixture between your palms (they should be around the size of a 20p piece) and arrange them a couple of centimetres apart on a plate lined with greaseproof paper. You may need wet hands to do this, as it can be a little sticky. Place the bites in the freezer for 90 minutes to harden.

As the bites are chilling, melt the white chocolate in a heatproof bowl over a saucepan of boiling water, or in a microwave in 20-second bursts, stirring in between so it doesn't burn . Take it off the heat and let it cool slightly.

Remove the bites from the freezer, let them soften for a few minutes and re-roll into spheres (they will have flattened as they froze).

Using a teaspoon or fork to hold them, dip the bites one by one in the cooled chocolate. Move fast – you don't want the filling to go too soft – and place each one back on the greaseproof paper. Use a cocktail stick to tidy the edges and create a neat swirl on top.

Put the bites back in the freezer for 90 minutes to set. They should keep for a week in the fridge.

CASHEW NUT BRITTLE

SERVES 6-8

Like honeycomb or boiled sweets, nut brittle is one of those treats that seems to serve no other purpose than to rot your teeth – but boy does it taste good. I add butter to mine to give it a salty kick, and use big, creamy cashews instead of the standard peanuts.

150g caster sugar	2 tablespoons salted butter	100g raw, unsalted cashews (or other nuts if you prefer)

Optional: sugar thermometer

Prepare a surface for your brittle to set by covering a chopping board in a sheet of greaseproof paper.

Put the sugar in a pan over a low heat and let it caramelize. Don't stir – just gently tilt the pan from side to side if it looks like it's heating unevenly (stirring can cause crystals to form). It should take around 6 minutes to melt and turn golden brown. If you've got a sugar thermometer, it should reach around 150°C (called 'hard crack' stage).

At this point, add the butter. It will sizzle and foam but should settle down and continue to caramelize. Keep the heat low so it doesn't burn.

Once the foaming has stopped, add the cashew nuts. It's important that these are raw, as the caramelized sugar is extremely hot and will start to cook the nuts; if you use ready-roasted ones, there's a risk they'll burn.

Stir the nuts around until they're completely coated in the caramel, and let them cook for another 3 to 4 minutes.

Tip the brittle on to the prepared surface and use a spatula to spread out the nuts, making sure they're evenly dispersed throughout the caramel.

Leave it to set for 1 to 2 hours, then use a hammer or rolling pin to smash it into pieces. You may need to cover the brittle with another sheet of greaseproof paper first – or shield your eyes! It'll keep crunchy and delicious for 4 days in a sealed tin.

 TIP: *If you have some to hand, sprinkle a pinch of coarse sea salt over the finished brittle.*

SALTED CHOCOLATE FUDGE

MAKES AROUND 40 PIECES

Salty and sweet is one of my favourite flavour combinations, and it works well in this rich, bittersweet fudge. It makes a great gift, too, wrapped in baking paper and tied with a ribbon – either individual chunks, or as a giant slab.

50g salted butter (buy the saltiest you can find – my favourite is Kerrygold), cut into cubes	360g dark chocolate chips or chopped chocolate	1 x 397ml tin of sweetened condensed milk

Square baking tray (25cm x 25cm)

Put the butter and the chocolate chips in a medium-sized heatproof bowl. Microwave for 2 minutes on high, stirring every 30 seconds, until both have melted, or melt in a heatproof bowl over a saucepan of boiling water.

Pour in the condensed milk and heat again for another 2 minutes, stirring halfway. Stir the mixture – which should now be quite thick – thoroughly with a metal spoon.

Line your baking tray with aluminium foil (this is better than greaseproof paper as it fits tightly into the corners) and pour in the molten fudge mixture. Place it in the fridge to set for 3 to 4 hours.

Cut the fudge into small squares and store in an airtight tin for up to a week. If you want it super-salty, sprinkle a little sea salt over the top.

CRUMBLY CARAMELS

MAKES 24 PIECES

Some people make these with cream or condensed milk, but I make mine with something you're far more likely to have in your fridge: milk. If you want an extra kick, try adding a pinch of chilli flakes, cardamom or sea salt – or shake in a handful of chopped pecans.

350g dark brown soft sugar	300ml semi-skimmed milk	100g salted butter

Square baking tray (25cm x 25cm)
Optional: sugar thermometer

Line the baking tray with greaseproof paper. Put all the ingredients in a heavy-bottomed saucepan and heat slowly, stirring constantly. When the sugar and butter have dissolved, turn the heat up high. Bring the mixture to the boil and simmer for 20 to 25 minutes.

When the mixture rises to the top of the pan, just before it overflows, take it off the heat and stir vigorously until the mixture comes back down. Place it back on the heat. Repeat this step as necessary until the mixture reaches 'soft ball' stage. This is the point between 112°C and 116°C on a sugar thermometer.

If you don't have a thermometer, check the caramel is ready by picking up a small amount on a teaspoon and dropping it into a glass of cold water. If it stays intact and forms a pliable ball, it's done. Repeat this step every few minutes to check.

Take the mixture off the heat and allow it to stand for 1 to 2 minutes. Then, using a whisk, beat it for 5 minutes until it loses its gloss and starts to thicken. Quickly pour it into the baking tray and leave to set at room temperature. This should take around 2 hours. Once set, cut the crumbly caramels into small squares.

 TIP: *For an easy way to clean all that sticky mixture off your pan and utensils, simply fill the pan to the brim with boiling water, dunk all the utensils in it – and leave for 5 minutes. The sugar will re-dissolve in the water, leaving everything shiny and clean.*

MANGO ROLL-UPS

MAKES 5 ROLL-UPS

These retro goodies are perfect for kids' lunchboxes – or a healthy snack in the office. There's no added sugar, just a tiny squirt of honey, and the rest is all-natural golden fruit.

1 large ripe mango (around 500g)	2 teaspoons lemon juice	2 teaspoons runny honey

Preheat the oven to 100°C/80°C fan.

Line a large baking sheet with greaseproof paper. Make sure it's tightly pressed into the corners: you want a nice even rectangle.

Peel and de-stone the mango and put all the fruit, juice and pulp you can eke out of the skin into a blender. Add the lemon juice and honey (be generous with your teaspoons). Whizz everything together for a couple of minutes until you have a smooth purée.

Tip the mixture out on to the lined baking sheet, and smooth out to a very thin, even layer (around 2–3mm thick) using a palette knife or the back of a spoon.

Place in the oven and bake at a low heat for 3 to 4 hours. You'll know it's ready when the purée has fully dried out and is soft and pliable to the touch. If it's still looking too wet, turn the heat up a fraction towards the end of the cooking time.

Before it starts to cool, place another sheet of greaseproof paper on top and peel the mixture off the sheet it was baked on. Press the paper down firmly (or use a rolling pin if you need to) so the fruit sticks, then use a sharp knife to even out the edges into a neat rectangle.

Roll the whole rectangle up into a cylinder, and snip it into five pieces. Your roll-ups are ready to eat! They should keep for around a week.

 TIP: *Experiment with other fruit instead of mango: 1 medium pineapple, 5 or 6 green apples, 1 honeydew melon or 2 handfuls of mixed berries.*

HONEYCOMB

SERVES 6–8

Cinder toffee, hokey pokey, sea foam … call it what you will, but it's hard to better these deliciously decadent golden shards. You can crumble it into pieces and mix it into ice cream or pile it high on a cake, or keep your honeycomb chunky and munch it like sweets.

200g caster sugar	5 tablespoons golden syrup	2 teaspoons bicarbonate of soda

Square baking tray (25cm x 25cm)

Line the baking tray, greasing both on top of and underneath the greaseproof paper. The greasing is really important here, otherwise the honeycomb will stick fast to the tray.

Pour the sugar and syrup into a large, deep saucepan. To make the syrup easier to handle (and the spoon easier to clean), I wipe the spoon with a drop of sunflower oil first. Stirring constantly with a wooden spoon, heat the mixture gently so the sugar crystals dissolve.

Once the sugar is dissolved, turn the heat up and let the mixture bubble. You want it to turn a nice amber colour – and as soon as it does, turn off the heat.

Add the bicarbonate of soda to the mixture and stir quickly. It should foam and expand in size quite rapidly – but don't worry, this is entirely normal. Working quickly, tip the honeycomb into the baking tray. Be careful – it will be super-hot.

Handle the tray gently once you've got all the honeycomb in, as you want to keep that nice light, bubbly texture. It takes around 1 to 2 hours to cool, after which it's ready to eat.

I use the end of a rolling pin to break mine into pieces, but you can use any kitchen implement – or, if you're like the lovely Mary Berry, a quick karate chop of the hand.

The honeycomb will keep for 2 to 3 days in a sealed tin.

TIP: *If you want it to last even longer, dip it in chocolate (dark or milk) once it's cool. It will keep for up to a month – and taste sweeter still!*

NO-BAKE COCO BALLS

MAKES 24 BALLS

These crowd-pleasing petit-fours are rich, tropical and sweet. Dates are a great raw baking ingredient, binding everything together as well as taking the place of sugar. You don't even have to bake them – so you can whip up a batch in minutes.

100g dark chocolate	180g pitted dates	4 tablespoons desiccated coconut

Weigh out half the chocolate and chop it into small chunks. Put these in a food processor along with the dates and the coconut. Whiz the ingredients until they come together into a crumbly ball.

Take the mixture out of the food processor and roll small balls – no bigger than 50p pieces – between your palms. Place them on a plate covered with greaseproof paper.

Melt the remainder of the chocolate in a heatproof bowl by blasting it for 20-second bursts in the microwave, or put it over a pan of boiling water and stir.

Let the melted chocolate cool slightly. As it does, prepare a piping bag by snipping a minuscule corner off a sandwich bag (no more than a millimetre or two – you want to create a pinhole).

Use a spatula to transfer the cooled chocolate to the piping bag – being careful to hold the open end shut until you're ready to use it – and drizzle it over the coco balls. Don't worry about making a pattern – the messier, the better. If all this sounds like too much work, you can be lazy and drizzle the chocolate from a spoon – but it won't look as professional.

Once the chocolate has set, put the balls in paper petit-four cases to serve.

SQUIDGY CHOCOLATE TRUFFLES

MAKES 24 TRUFFLES

Devilishly decadent, these truffles are the perfect after-dinner treat. There's a tang from the cream cheese, bitterness from the cocoa and a yummy squidgy centre – and they're (ever so slightly) healthier than your average truffles made from double cream.

230g dark chocolate	1 x 180g tub of low-fat cream cheese	10g cocoa powder

Melt the chocolate in a heatproof bowl in 20-second bursts in the microwave, or over a saucepan of boiling water. In a separate bowl, whisk the cream cheese with a fork until it is soft.

Add a spoonful of the melted chocolate to the cream cheese, and stir it in. Then, add the whole cream cheese mixture to the bowl containing the chocolate. Doing it this way round stops the mixture from going lumpy, which is a risk if you add anything cold to warm chocolate.

Cover the truffle mix with cling film and place it in the fridge until it solidifies. It should take 1 to 2 hours. When it's nearly ready, sift the cocoa powder on to a plate.

Roll up your sleeves – it's going to get messy. Lift fingerfuls of the truffle mixture and roll them into balls (around the size of a grape) between your palms. Put each ball into the pile of cocoa powder and roll it around until it's fully covered. Place the truffles on a baking sheet or large plate lined with greaseproof paper.

If you're in a hurry, stick the truffles in the fridge to chill. If not, leave them in a cool place for an hour to set. They're nice when they're still a little gooey, and should keep in a tin for a week.

 TIP: *Instead of cocoa powder, use desiccated coconut, chocolate sprinkles or chopped pistachios to coat your truffles.*

PEPPERMINT SHARDS

SERVES 6–8

These sugary shards have the texture of boiled sweets, but rather than break your teeth they stick in them like toffee. I love bashing the shiny sheet of caramel with a rolling pin at the end – just make sure you've got plenty of room, as sharp missiles can fly everywhere.

140g granulated sugar	7 tablespoons corn syrup or agave nectar (corn syrup will give you a clear finish, agave will be amber-coloured – but the taste is the same)	3 teaspoons peppermint extract

Optional: sugar thermometer

Prepare a chopping board or baking tray for your shards to set. I use a sheet of aluminium foil underneath a sheet of greaseproof paper – this way you can turn up the edges of the foil to stop the mixture running off the sides.

Put the sugar and syrup or nectar in a saucepan over a medium heat. As the mixture heats it will froth and bubble, so keep stirring it to stop it sticking to the pan. If it looks like it's starting to caramelize, take it off the heat for a few seconds.

Continue heating until the temperature rises to between 150°C and 180°C – what is known as the 'hard crack' stage. Use a sugar thermometer if you have one. If not, just keep it on the heat until it's been bubbling and frothing for around 7 minutes.

When the mixture is sufficiently hot, take the saucepan off the heat. The sugar should have dissolved and, underneath all the froth, it should be transparent. Add the peppermint extract and mix thoroughly.

Tip the mixture on to the greaseproof paper and use a palette knife to spread it out to a few millimetres thick. Leave to set for a couple of hours, before covering with another sheet of greaseproof paper and bashing with a rolling pin to split it into shards.

The shards are perfect as an after-dinner treat – you can even dip them in dark chocolate to make your own version of After Eights. Store in an airtight tin lined with greaseproof paper.

 TIP: *You can use food colouring instead of mint extract to create multicoloured boiled-sweet shards, though it really only works with clear corn syrup. Simply follow the method as above and add the food colouring at the end, mixing only slightly to create a rippled, tie-dye effect.*

BREAD

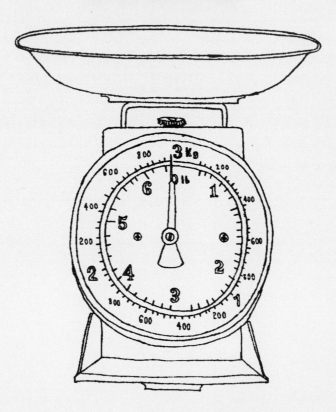

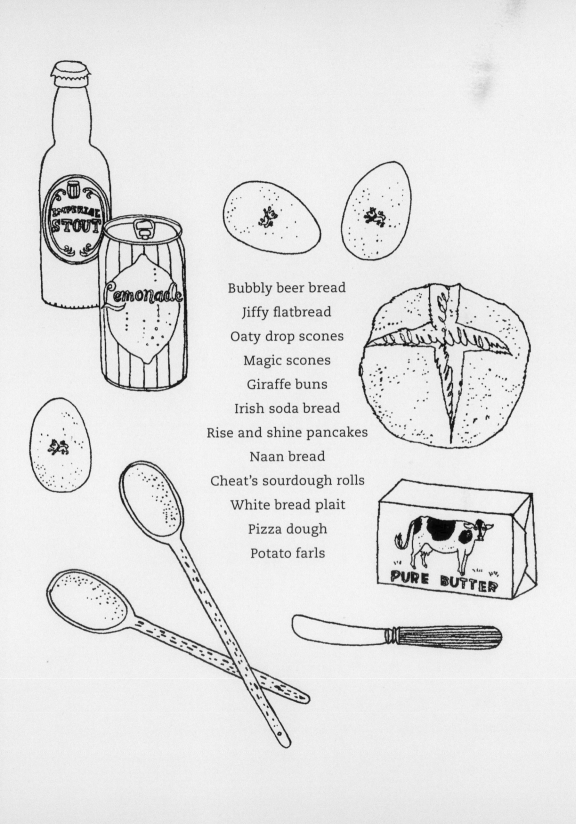

Bubbly beer bread

Jiffy flatbread

Oaty drop scones

Magic scones

Giraffe buns

Irish soda bread

Rise and shine pancakes

Naan bread

Cheat's sourdough rolls

White bread plait

Pizza dough

Potato farls

BUBBLY BEER BREAD

SERVES 8-10

This is a very hands-on dough, so be ready to roll your sleeves up and dig right on in. It's rich, hoppy and malty, and goes down a treat with a slab of butter and a hearty stew on a chilly day.

380g self-raising flour, plus a pinch for dusting	100g caster sugar	1 x 330ml can or bottle of dark beer

Standard loaf tin (22cm x 12cm x 7cm) – or you can bake it free-form on a baking sheet

Preheat the oven to 200°C/180°C fan, and grease and line the loaf tin.

Sift the flour into a mixing bowl, and add the sugar followed by the beer. Pour the beer in gradually so it doesn't froth too much. Mix everything together using a wooden spoon, and transfer the dough to the tin.

If you'd prefer to bake it free-form, make a 'bowl' out of circular layers of aluminium foil and place the dough inside this on a flat baking sheet lined with greaseproof paper. It is a very sloppy dough and can't support itself, so make sure there are no gaps for it to seep out.

Dust the top with a little flour before putting it in the oven. Bake the loaf for 45 to 50 minutes. You'll know it's done when the crust on top turns golden (and you can stick a skewer down the centre of the loaf to check the inside is cooked through).

Turn out on to a wire rack to cool.

 TIP: *If you can't get your hands on a dark beer, pale ale will do just fine – but the flavour will be a little sharper and less malty. You can even use a can of lemonade for a slightly sweet, slightly salted loaf that goes well with cheese.*

JIFFY FLATBREAD

MAKES 8 FLATBREADS

This flatbread got its name because you can literally make it in a jiffy. If you're looking for something to soak up an oily Greek salad or dunk in a bowl of hummus, cook up a batch of this savoury unleavened bread in a hot griddle pan.

300g white spelt flour, plus extra for dusting	1 teaspoon bicarbonate of soda	6 egg whites

Griddle pan

Cut eight small squares (around 10cm x 10cm) of greaseproof paper and put aside. Sift the flour and bicarbonate of soda into a bowl. In a separate bowl, whisk the egg whites roughly with a fork, then add them to the flour mixture. Mix until it comes together into a soft dough. Place it in the fridge for half an hour to firm up.

Turn the dough out on to a well-floured surface and split it into eight pieces. Roll each piece out into a thin flatbread – it doesn't matter what shape; part of the joy of flatbread is that it's made from misshapen lumps of dough – but make sure they're all the same thickness, no more than half a centimetre.

Place each flatbread on a square of greaseproof paper and stack them on top of one another. Use plenty of flour to handle them so they don't break.

Put the griddle pan over a high heat on the hob. Check its temperature by letting a drop of water fall into the pan – if it sizzles and evaporates immediately, it's hot enough. Once the pan is ready, wipe it with kitchen paper to dry it off so there's no liquid in the pan. Transfer the flatbreads to the hot pan, one by one. Let them cook for 3 to 4 minutes on each side until they harden and puff up, then flip and repeat on the other side. There should be dark scorch marks criss-crossing each flatbread. Serve hot and, if you want, drizzled with melted butter, sea salt and chopped fresh parsley.

 TIP: *Spelt is a sweet, nutty flour – you can also use ordinary white flour but it won't be as flavoursome, so you might need to add a few pinches of sugar.*

OATY DROP SCONES

EACH BATCH (6 DROP SCONES) SERVES 2–3

These drop scones are like a healthy version of the American breakfast classic: blueberry pancakes. They're stodgy, packed full of protein and bursting with purple jewels of fruit. I eat mine with rashers of streaky bacon and a drizzle of maple syrup.

6 egg whites	200g rolled oats (you can use flavoured oats instead, or even finely milled muesli)	1 punnet fresh blueberries (around 200g)

Whisk the egg whites gently by hand for a couple of minutes until they start to froth. This keeps the drop scones light and airy.

Pour in the oats, and stir to combine. If the mixture seems a little dry, add one more whisked egg white – it all depends on the size of your eggs. Add around three-quarters of the blueberries, and stir.

Meanwhile, heat a knob of butter in a large frying pan and get it really hot. Spoon the drop scone mix into the pan (you can probably fit around three in a triangle shape), flatten it into a 1cm-thick circle and let it sizzle away for 4 to 5 minutes.

Peek underneath: you'll know it's ready when it's golden brown and the oats are sticking together. Use a fish slice to flip each drop scone over, and repeat on the other side.

Tip the finished scones out on to a plate and serve hot, topped with the remaining blueberries. If you're making a bigger batch, keep your drop scones hot on a plate in a low oven, sandwiched between circles of greaseproof paper so they don't go soggy.

MAGIC SCONES

MAKES 10 LARGE SCONES

This is one of those recipes you really have to try for yourself before you believe it works. I defy anyone to tell these fluffy scones apart from the originals, especially when laden with strawberry jam and clotted cream.

600g self-raising flour, plus extra for dusting	300ml double cream	1 x 330ml can of lemonade

7cm fluted round cutter

Preheat the oven to 220°C/200°C fan.

Sift the flour into a mixing bowl. Slowly add the cream, followed by the can of lemonade. Stir the mixture together using a metal spoon. I try to avoid using a wooden spoon, as a metal one cuts through the mixture better.

Use your hands to bring the dough together, and shape it into a ball in the bowl, adding a few more tablespoons of flour if it's too sticky. Working quickly (so it keeps its shape), turn it out on to a heavily floured surface and knead it lightly.

Pat the dough to a thickness of around 4cm and cut into circles using the cutter or, if you don't have one, the rim of a clean glass or small mug (you'll lose the pleats, but it's better than nothing).

Put the scones on a baking sheet lined with greaseproof paper, around 3cm apart, neatening them up using a wet knife if necessary.

Bake in the oven for 20 minutes. Give them another few minutes if the tops haven't turned golden brown. Allow to cool on a wire rack.

 TIP: *You can top the scones with easy, three-ingredient jam. Put 500g of fresh raspberries and 500g of caster sugar in a pan, heat until it boils, and add 1 teaspoon of butter. Let the mixture bubble away for 10 minutes until it gets a jam-like consistency – then cool.*

GIRAFFE BUNS

MAKES 6 BUNS

This bread alternative might not look like much in the mixing bowl, but just wait until you put it in the oven: the crust crackles and comes out looking like a giraffe's golden coat. It's a light, spongy bun that you can eat on its own or stuff with sandwich fillings.

3 eggs	½ teaspoon cream of tartar	80g low-fat cream cheese

Preheat the oven to 200°C/180°C fan, and line two baking sheets with grease-proof paper.

Separate the eggs into two bowls and whisk the whites with the cream of tartar until they form stiff peaks. This should take several minutes with an electric whisk.

Slightly soften the cream cheese by microwaving it for 10 seconds or leaving it out of the fridge for an hour before baking.

Mix it into the egg yolks until fully combined. Slowly add the whipped whites to the egg yolk mixture, a little at a time, folding with a metal spoon to combine the ingredients without over-mixing.

When it's all come together, use a ladle to dollop the mixture on to the baking sheets, a good 5cm apart. The mixture is quite liquid, so the buns will spread.

Bake for 20 to 22 minutes, or until the bread has puffed up and formed a mottled crust. Let the buns cool completely on the baking sheets.

They will keep in a sealed container for 3 to 4 days. Simply pop them carefully in the toaster or under the grill for a few minutes to freshen them up.

IRISH SODA BREAD

SERVES 8–10

Warming, fluffy and delicious, this soda bread reminds me of my childhood. No Ulster fry was ever complete without a wedge on the side, loaded with melting butter. You can eat it for breakfast, lunch or dinner – and pretty much every time in between.

450g self-raising flour	2 teaspoons bicarbonate of soda	300ml buttermilk (or, to make your own, use 285ml normal milk, add 1 tablespoon lemon juice and whisk thoroughly)

Preheat the oven to 240°C/220°C fan.

Sift the flour and bicarbonate of soda into a bowl. Add the buttermilk, and mix. Try to get rid of the lumps without overworking the mixture, which will stop the bread from rising properly in the oven.

Once it comes together into a dough, stick your hands into the bowl and turn it out on to a floured surface. Roll the dough over a couple of times, then shape it into a round and gently flatten until it's about 5cm thick.

Transfer to a lightly greased baking tray and, using a serrated knife, mark a large cross on the top as if to divide the loaf into four quarters. The cut should go around 0.5cm deep into the loaf.

Place in the hot oven for the first 10 minutes, then lower the temperature to 190°C/170°C fan for a further 20 minutes. Stick a skewer into the centre of the loaf to check it is cooked through. If it comes out sticky, give the bread another 5 minutes until the skewer is clean.

Remove from the oven and place on a cooling rack. Slice when cool, and serve with butter, cheese or jam.

RISE AND SHINE PANCAKES

EACH BATCH (2 PANCAKES) SERVES 1

I can't get enough of these paleo – or caveman – pancakes, which are made from the same simple ingredients our ancestors used to eat hundreds of thousands of years ago. They're the ultimate easy breakfast treat, and you can whiz up a batch in minutes.

1 large egg	½ teaspoon ground cinnamon	1 red apple

Beat the egg in a medium bowl, and add the cinnamon.

Peel and very finely grate the apple into the egg mixture, and blend well. Leave the mixture aside for at least half an hour to thicken (but cover it tightly with cling film to stop the apple turning brown).

When you're ready to cook the pancakes, heat a knob of butter in a medium frying pan. Drop the batter into the pan, in blobs of two heaped tablespoons a few centimetres apart, and cook over a medium heat until the pancakes are lightly browned underneath. It shouldn't take more than 2 to 3 minutes.

Turn the pancakes over using a fish slice or palette knife (or flip if you're feeling brave) and cook for another few minutes on the other side. Turn out on to a plate to serve.

The pancakes are easiest to make per serving, so you don't have to fiddle around trying to get exactly half an egg or half an apple in the pan. Just multiply the ingredients to match the number of people who are eating – and double up if they're feeling hungry.

Serve the pancakes with natural yoghurt and some more grated apple, icing sugar or chopped nuts.

 TIP: *You can also use a small mashed banana in place of the apple, and grated dark chocolate, desiccated coconut or instant coffee dissolved in water instead of cinnamon (1 teaspoon each).*

NAAN BREAD

MAKES 4 SMALL NAANS

Traditionally cooked in a tandoori – a cylindrical clay oven – this grilled naan bread might lack panache in technique, but it's still the same buttery, puffed dough, which you can flavour with garlic or herbs and use to soak up the spiciest of curries.

250g self-raising flour, plus extra for kneading	130ml semi-skimmed milk	3 tablespoons salted butter, melted

Sift the flour into a bowl and slowly add the milk, followed by 2 tablespoons of the butter. Stir together and, using your hands, bring the mixture together into a firm dough.

Sprinkle a little more flour over a flat surface, turn the dough out on to it and knead for approximately 10 minutes, until it's smooth and elastic. Leave the dough in an oiled bowl covered with a tea towel for an hour. This kicks the raising agent into action and helps the butter seep into the dough.

Split the dough into four equal-sized balls and roll them out to around 0.5cm thick. Naan bread is normally served in teardrop shapes, so aim for this – just make one end slightly fatter than the other.

Preheat the grill to medium and put a baking sheet under to heat up.

Transfer the naans to the baking sheet and brush them with the remaining table-spoon of butter. Grill them for 15 minutes until brown and puffed up. Flip them over and give them another 5 minutes on the other side.

Eat them hot, topped with whatever you want – desiccated coconut, more melted butter, garlic, chopped herbs – or just a big dollop of meat and sauce.

CHEAT'S SOURDOUGH ROLLS

MAKES 12 ROLLS

These little puffs of air are the definition of store-cupboard baking. I guarantee you'll have all the ingredients easily to hand – and you can rustle them up in under half an hour. I like to eat mine hot, with butter, on the side of a steaming bowl of tomato soup.

240g self-raising flour	200ml semi-skimmed milk	5 tablespoons mayonnaise

Preheat the oven to 200°C/180°C fan. Grease two baking sheets and line with greaseproof paper.

Sift the flour into a bowl and slowly add the milk, stirring constantly. Add the mayonnaise and mix vigorously to get rid of any lumps.

The batter should be thick but runny, and when you lift your spoon out, you should be able to see elastic threads forming – this is the raising agent in the flour starting to get to work.

Drop heaped dessert spoons of the mixture on to the baking sheets, spacing them 4–5cm apart. Use the spoon to try to round off the edges and neaten the tops.

Bake for 30 to 35 minutes, or until they've risen and are just starting to go brown on top. Swap the trays halfway through the cooking time to ensure they're evenly cooked. Don't worry if the rolls look a little knobbly and misshapen – this all adds to the rustic look.

Cool on a wire rack before serving. The rolls should keep for up to 4 days in an airtight tin – and you can even freeze them; just remember to use within 1 month.

WHITE BREAD PLAIT

SERVES 12–14

Freshly baked bread is one of the greatest smells on the planet – right up there with just-mown grass and mulled wine at Christmas. All you need for this easy three-ingredient loaf is a little bit of time – don't rush it – and nimble fingers to arrange it into a pretty plait.

600g strong white bread flour	14g (2 x 7g sachets) fast-action dried yeast	400ml cool water

Sift the flour into a bowl and add the yeast. Give it a quick stir. Add around half the water, using your hands to move the mixture around.

Slowly add the remainder of the water, a slug at a time, combining it with the dry ingredients as you go. You might not need all the water to get the dough to the right consistency (I usually have around a tablespoon left at the end). You want the dough to be tacky, rather than sticky or wet.

Once the dough feels right, turn it on to a surface greased lightly with olive oil. Put a dot of oil in the palm of each hand and rub them together so they're slightly oily too.

Use the heels of your hands to push the dough into the table and away from you at the same time. After a few kneads, it should make an oblong shape. Fold this in half, left to right, then rotate the dough so the opening is at the bottom again. Repeat.

It should take around 5 to 10 minutes for the dough to become smooth and elastic. Grease the inside of a large bowl with a little more oil, and put the ball of kneaded dough inside. Lightly grease one side of a piece of cling film and put this on top.

Leave the bowl in a warm place (beside the hob or above the oven if possible) for up to 3 hours, or until the dough has doubled in size.

Uncover the dough and knock the air out of it by shaping it into a fat oblong. Use a sharp knife to divide it into three equal pieces and roll each into a thin sausage shape, around 40cm long.

Squash the ends together, separate out the three strands and plait them as you would a ponytail. When you get to the other end, squash them together again and neaten the whole thing up.

Carefully lift the plaited loaf on to a baking sheet lined with greaseproof paper. Place a sheet of cling film, lightly oiled, over the top and allow the dough to rise again for another hour. You'll know it's ready when the dough is springy: push your finger into it and watch it bounce back.

Preheat the oven to 240°C/220°C fan. Half-fill a baking tray with boiling water and place it on the lower shelf of the oven. The steam helps crisp up the crust.

Bake the bread for 40 minutes, or until it's golden and sounds hollow when you tap the base. Allow it to cool on a wire rack. Slice while fresh and enjoy with a slab of salty butter or Brie.

PIZZA DOUGH

MAKES 1 LARGE PIZZA

Make like an Italian with this easy-as-pie pizza dough. You can add whatever toppings you want, prepare it ahead of time and even freeze it for another day. 'Buon appetito!'

210g self-raising flour, plus a few extra tablespoons for dusting	220g low-fat Greek yoghurt	2 tablespoons olive oil

Optional: pizza stone

Sift the flour into a bowl and add the Greek yoghurt. Mix with a wooden spoon, and add the olive oil. Stir to combine. Once the mixture starts coming together, roll your sleeves up and use your hands to bring the dough into a smooth ball.

Turn it out on to a floured surface and knead for 5 to 10 minutes, adding more flour if the dough becomes too sticky. Place the ball of dough in the fridge for at least an hour to firm up.

Preheat the oven to 220°C/200°C fan, with a baking tray or pizza stone inside.

When the dough is ready, place it on a sheet of baking paper, roll it out into a 0.5cm-thick circle (coat your rolling pin in plenty of flour to stop it sticking) and start adding your toppings.

Slide the pizza (plus baking paper) across on to the preheated baking tray or pizza stone and cook for 25 to 30 minutes. If you used a tray, remove it from under the pizza and place it one shelf down so the base can crisp up for the last 10 minutes.

The pizza is ready when the cheese has melted, the crust has browned and the toppings are sizzling hot.

 TIP: *To turn this into a decadent dessert, leave out the olive oil, make the dough as normal and spread 200g Nutella over the top before baking to create a sweet, chocolaty pizza.*

POTATO FARLS

MAKES 8 FARLS

Much like soda bread, these potato farls were a staple of my childhood. I love the notion of replacing flour with starchy potatoes; the result is deliciously filling. Eat these little triangles hot, spread with butter and topped with a sprinkle of sea salt.

2 large potatoes (roughly 350g), peeled and chopped	100g plain flour, plus a little extra for cooking	1 tablespoon salted butter, melted

Parboil the potatoes for around 20 minutes in a saucepan of boiling water. Once they're soft, drain them and leave them in a colander for a few minutes to dry off, then put them back in the pan and mash until smooth. Allow to cool slightly.

Sift the flour into a bowl and add the mashed potatoes, followed by the melted butter. Mix well until everything comes together into a firm dough.

Turn this dough out on to a sheet of baking paper and roll it into a circle around 0.5cm thick. Slice the circle into eight wedges (as you would a pizza).

Heat a large frying pan over a medium heat and, as it warms up, sprinkle a little flour over the base of the pan. Cook the potato farls, two at a time, for 3 to 4 minutes on each side, or until they puff up and start steaming. Wipe out the pan and replace the flour between each bake – otherwise it will burn.

Eat immediately, or reheat later by popping them back in the pan or in the toaster like a normal slice of bread. Store wrapped in aluminium foil or covered in the fridge for up to 4 days.

SAVOURY
BAKES

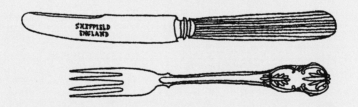

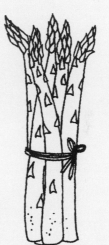

Parmesan crispbreads

Cauliflower wraps

Sweetcorn fritters

Smoked salmon soufflés

Pumpkin patties

Ham and cheese pinwheels

Crustless quiche

Broccoli falafels

Asparagus tartlets

Bacon breakfast cups

Nutty nibbles

Cheesy crêpes

Goats in blankets

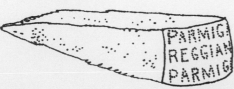

PARMESAN CRISPBREADS

MAKES 20–25 SMALL CRISPBREADS

Like posh Mini Cheddars, these little rounds of cheesy goodness will transport you back to your childhood. You can make them sophisticated and serve them with dips, cheese or pâté, but most likely they'll be long gone before you get them to the plate.

140g plain flour	125g salted butter, cubed	120g Parmesan or other hard cheese, grated

5cm fluted round cutter

Sift the flour into a bowl and add the cubes of butter. Rub the two together using your fingers, until the mixture resembles breadcrumbs.

Add the grated Parmesan, holding back 1 large tablespoon for topping the crispbreads, and bring everything together into a dough. Cover with cling film and chill in the fridge for an hour.

Place the chilled dough on a clean, dry surface. Using a rolling pin (and a sheet of greaseproof paper if the dough is sticky), roll the dough out to a thickness of 1cm.

Preheat the oven to 200°C/180°C fan.

Cut out rounds using the cutter and place on a baking tray lined with greaseproof paper, spaced a few centimetres apart. Sprinkle with the remaining Parmesan.

Bake for 15 minutes, until crisp and golden. Cool on a wire rack.

CAULIFLOWER WRAPS

EACH BATCH (8 WRAPS) SERVES 4

These are my guilt-free garlic bread – light, mini tortilla-style wraps made from crumbled cauliflower, garlic and a little bit of egg to bind. They taste great alongside spicy chicken thighs and roasted veg, or dunked in a hot curry.

1 whole cauliflower	3 eggs	2 teaspoons mashed garlic (I use garlic paste straight from a jar – shh! – but if you're mashing your own, it's around 3 cloves)

Preheat the oven to 220°C/200°C fan, and line two large baking sheets with greaseproof paper. Cut the stalks and leaves off the cauliflower and place the florets in a blender. Blitz into crumbs in batches. Don't discard the stalks – you can eat them later.

Tip the crumbs into a heatproof bowl and microwave on full power for 2 minutes, stirring every 30 seconds. Stop once they've softened and are piping hot.

Mix the cauli with the eggs in a bowl, and stir in the garlic. Whisk the mixture until it is relatively smooth – you want it quite thick but not lumpy. Place dollops of the mixture (two dessert spoons each) on to the baking sheets, at least 10cm apart. Use the back of the spoon to spread them into flat circles, around ½cm thick.

Bake for around 10 minutes, flip them over using a fish slice and bake for another 6 minutes. You'll know they're done when they're just starting to colour on either side – don't over-bake them or they'll turn hard and crispy.

When you're ready to serve the wraps, heat a knob of butter in a really hot frying pan and sear for 2 to 3 minutes on each side until they crisp up and the edges start to catch. Eat them hot, on the side of your meal, like a wrap or naan bread.

 TIP: *Swap the garlic for curry powder, paprika or herby za'atar (a delicious Middle Eastern herb mix made from oregano, sumac, cumin and marjoram) to make your wraps nice and spicy.*

SWEETCORN FRITTERS

These crispy veggie bakes take just minutes to make and taste so good. The sweet kernels of corn, salty cheese and eggy base are a mouthwatering combination. I like to eat mine for breakfast, topped with bacon and avocado, or on the side of a juicy steak for tea.

160g tinned sweetcorn, drained	50g hard cheese (I use Cheddar but you can use any hard cheese, such as Parmesan, pecorino, Gruyère or Gouda)	2 eggs

Tip the sweetcorn kernels into a bowl.

Grate the cheese on the finest side of the grater. You want it to be as flour-like as possible: this is what binds the fritters together. Add the grated cheese and the eggs to the sweetcorn, and stir vigorously to combine.

Heat a teaspoon of olive oil in a large saucepan over a medium heat.

Ladle spoonfuls of the sweetcorn mix (around the size of two dessert spoons) into the pan, leaving a couple of centimetres between them as they may spread a little.

Cook for 3 to 4 minutes on each side until set and golden brown, flipping the fritters with a fish slice. If there's a little too much liquid in the pan, drain it off in between batches – you want them nice and crisp. Serve the fritters hot, straight from the pan.

 TIP: *These fritters taste great sprinkled with chilli flakes or squeezed with the juice of a lime.*

SMOKED SALMON SOUFFLÉS

MAKES 6 SOUFFLÉS

Soufflés have a reputation for being fiddly and impossible to get right. But recently chefs have revealed the secret to making them perfectly every time: ready-made custard. My little cheat's smoked salmon soufflés are like fluffy clouds and will wow at any dinner party.

5 egg whites	100g smoked salmon	150g shop-bought fresh custard (not the fancy kind – you don't want it to taste sweet)

6 small ramekins, teacups or soufflé dishes

Preheat the oven to 220°C/200°C fan. Grease the ramekins with a little butter and arrange them in a deep baking tray, ready to fill.

Whisk the egg whites until they form stiff peaks.

Put 80g of the salmon into a separate bowl and use a fork to break it up into small pieces. Add the custard, mix and leave to infuse for 30 minutes.

Using a metal spoon, slowly fold the egg whites into the custard mixture, a spoonful at a time. Mix gently until no lumps of egg white remain and it's all combined.

Spoon the mixture into the ramekins, ensuring that there is an even distribution of salmon between them. Fill each one around two-thirds full and smooth out the top using the back of a spoon.

Make a bain-marie by pouring boiling water into the baking tray around the ramekins, until it comes around a third of the way up the outside of each one.

Bake the soufflés for 15 to 18 minutes, or until they have risen at least 2.5cm above the rim of the ramekin and are golden brown on top. Rotate the baking tray halfway through the cooking time to make sure they're evenly cooked.

Take the soufflés out of the tray (be careful – they're hot!) and serve immediately, scattered with the remainder of the salmon, lots of salt and freshly ground black pepper – and, if you really want to impress, a spoonful of soured cream and a sprinkle of chopped chives.

TIP: *You can even make these soufflés ahead of time. They'll keep in the fridge, covered in cling film, for up to 3 days. When it's time to serve, bake them for 10 minutes in a hot oven (240°C/220°C fan) to puff them up again – then garnish and get stuck in.*

PUMPKIN PATTIES

MAKES AROUND 18 SMALL PATTIES

These little savoury patties are delicious on the side of a bowl of soup or with a summery salad instead of a bread roll. The oats give the pumpkin flesh a nutty texture, enriched by the sprigs of herby thyme. I like to eat them hot, but they're good cold, too.

800g peeled, deseeded and chopped pumpkin (or you can use butternut squash, depending on what's in season)	Handful of fresh thyme, leaves picked and finely chopped	150g rolled oats

Preheat the oven to 200°C/180°C fan, and line a deep baking tray with aluminium foil.

Spread the pumpkin out on the baking tray. Sprinkle the thyme over the pumpkin and place it in the oven to roast for half an hour. Leave the oven on once it's finished – you'll need it again.

When the pumpkin's ready, let it cool slightly before tipping it into a bowl and mashing with a potato masher. There should be lots of lovely natural juices from the pumpkin, but if you need a little bit more liquid, you can add a few glugs of olive oil at this stage.

Stir in the oats and mix well until combined. You want the mixture to be rollable – so if it's still too runny, add a few more oats. Roll the patties into balls (roughly the size of a 50p piece) and spread them out on a baking sheet lined with greaseproof paper.

Flatten them down with a fork before baking again for 20 minutes, or until just crispy on top. Use a fish slice to prise them off the baking sheet, and serve.

HAM AND CHEESE PINWHEELS

MAKES 10–12 PINWHEELS

It doesn't take rocket science to come up with these little swirls, made from odds and ends of leftover pizza dough and my favourite sandwich fillings. But they're surprisingly versatile, and would do as a lunchtime snack or with some veg on the side for dinner.

450g pizza dough (my three ingredient version on page xxx takes just minutes to whip up, or you can buy it straight from the supermarket)	200g smoked bacon lardons or pancetta	100g Cheddar (or another hard cheese)

Roll the pizza dough out to a large rectangle, around 30cm wide by 40cm long.

Cook the lardons or pancetta as you normally would – in a frying pan or under the grill – and allow to cool before scattering them over the dough.

Grate the cheese and scatter over too, making sure you spread the fillings right to either side but a few centimetres short of the top and bottom, as you'll need some extra dough here.

Starting at the bottom edge, roll the pizza dough upwards into a tight cylinder, making sure you keep the fillings inside. Secure the outer edge by squeezing it together to seal everything in. Put the sausage of dough in the fridge for 30 minutes or so to firm up.

Preheat the oven to 200°C/180°C fan, and line a baking sheet with greaseproof paper. Using a sharp knife, cut the chilled dough into 1cm-thick slices. Don't discard the ends – they might not look pretty but they'll still taste good. Lay the pinwheels flat on the baking sheet and bake for 30 minutes, or until the dough has crisped up and the cheese melted. Serve hot, with lots of ketchup.

CRUSTLESS QUICHE

SERVES 6

This quick and easy dinner dish has become a firm favourite in my house. Quiche minus a crust is essentially a glorified omelette (or frittata) – but slice this up with a dressed green salad on the side, and I promise you won't miss that pastry one bit.

260g fresh spinach	8 eggs	175ml double cream

Round pie dish (20cm across)

Preheat the oven to 200°C/180°C fan, and grease the pie dish with a little oil or butter.

Cook the spinach as you normally would – I bung the whole thing, packaging and all, into the microwave for a minute, piercing the bag a few times first to let the steam out. Put it in a colander to let all the water drain out. Spinach can be very wet when cooked, so use a spoon to press it down and get rid of every last drop.

Once the spinach is dry, spread it out on a chopping board and roughly chop it. Arrange three-quarters of the spinach in the bottom of the pie dish.

In a measuring jug, whisk the eggs and mix in the cream. Pour this mixture over the spinach, arranging the remaining greenery prettily on top. Bake for 45 minutes, or until a skewer inserted into the centre of the quiche comes out clean.

Eat the quiche hot or cold. It will keep for 3 to 4 days in the fridge.

 TIP: *For a healthier alternative, use chicken or vegetable stock instead of double cream. You can also replace the spinach with whatever vegetable you have in the house.*

BROCCOLI FALAFELS

MAKES 15 FALAFELS

These baked balls of veggie deliciousness are the perfect accompaniment to a meal – or serve them with dunking bowls of hummus and rich tomato sauce for a starter.

1 head of broccoli (around 300g)	100g dried herby breadcrumbs (use whatever flavour you want, but avoid plain if you want these to pack a punch – I like Gallo's garlic and parsley breadcrumbs)	2 eggs

Preheat the oven to 220°C/200°C fan, and line a baking sheet with aluminium foil.

Cut the florets off the broccoli and discard the stalks and leaves – but don't bin them; save them for tomorrow night's dinner.

Place the florets in a saucepan of boiling, slightly salted water over a medium heat and simmer for 8 to 10 minutes, or until the florets turn a luminous green colour.

Drain and place the florets in a blender. Blitz the broccoli into tiny pieces. Add to a bowl containing the breadcrumbs, and mix thoroughly. Crack in the eggs and stir until combined. The mixture should come together but not be too wet.

Slightly dampen your hands and roll dessert spoon-sized blobs of the broccoli mixture between your palms to form balls. Arrange them on the baking sheet.

Bake for 20 to 25 minutes, or until the balls are crisp and starting to turn golden. Enjoy the falafels hot or cold, or keep them in the fridge for up to 3 days.

ASPARAGUS
TARTLETS

1 x 215g ready-rolled
frozen puff pastry

+

100g fresh
asparagus tips

+

90g
Gruyère cheese

ASPARAGUS TARTLETS

These light, summery tartlets are a dinner-party staple. The tangy Swiss Gruyère goes perfectly with the green asparagus, while the puff pastry is pillowy and rich in butter.

1 x 215g ready-rolled frozen puff pastry	100g fresh asparagus tips	90g Gruyère cheese

Take the pastry out of the freezer to defrost. While it's coming to room temperature, prepare and cook the asparagus tips. I snip mine into three pieces and griddle for around 8 minutes with a little seasoning and olive oil. You'll know it's ready when it's juicy, tender and slightly chargrilled.

Use tongs to remove the asparagus from the pan, and keep the cooking liquid – you can use this to brush the tart cases.

Once the pastry has defrosted, roll it out to a flat rectangle (around 0.5cm thick and 16cm x 10cm) and use a sharp knife to divide it into four portions. Remove these from the original paper, which will be quite soggy by now, and space them a few centimetres apart on a new piece of greaseproof paper on a baking sheet.

Carefully draw a smaller rectangle around 1.5cm inside the edge of each tartlet, scoring and not cutting through the pastry. This marks the inner area where the filling will go – the edges will puff up in the oven. Dip a pastry brush in the oil left in the pan and brush it over the pastry rectangles.

Grate the cheese, and pile even portions in the inner rectangle of each tartlet. Arrange the asparagus on top, splitting it equally between the tartlets.

Put the tartlets in the fridge for 10 minutes to firm up. While they do, preheat the oven to 195°C/175°C fan.

Bake the tartlets for 35 minutes, or until the pastry is puffed up and golden. Use a fish slice to take each one off the baking sheet. They make a delicious starter, served hot or cold with a few green leaves on the side.

BACON BREAKFAST CUPS

EACH BATCH (2 BREAKFAST CUPS) SERVES 1

The ultimate student breakfast with a gourmet twist. Toast, crispy bacon and perfectly runny eggs – but as you've never seen them before …

3 rashers of smoked bacon – streaky or back, though streaky works better	2 slices of wholemeal bread	2 eggs

12-hole muffin tray

Preheat the oven to 200°C/180°C fan.

Cook the bacon until crispy – around 4 minutes each side – in a hot frying pan. Set aside on a piece of kitchen paper to get rid of the excess grease.

Very lightly toast the bread so it is just hot. Using a pint glass, cut a large circle from the centre of each slice.

Grease two holes of the muffin tray with a knob of butter or teaspoon of oil, and press the circles of bread down into the holes.

Once the bacon has cooled, use scissors to cut it into large chunks. Arrange the bacon bits in a layer over the bread in the muffin tin. Hold back a couple of pieces for serving.

Crack an egg on top of each breakfast cup, and bake for approximately 20 minutes, or until the egg whites have set. Use a spoon to carefully remove the cups from the muffin tin while still piping hot. Scatter over the remaining bacon and serve with the bread off-cuts, which you can dunk into the egg like soldiers.

I like to make these as a quick brekkie for one – but if you can bear to share, just multiply the quantities by the number of people.

NUTTY NIBBLES

MAKES AROUND 14 NIBBLES

These crackers use nuts as a flour substitute and a topping. They're fail-safe party nibbles, delicious with dips, cheese or on their own.

350g salted mixed nuts and seeds (I like to use a bag of Brazil nuts, hazelnuts, walnuts, sesame seeds and sunflower seeds)	1 egg	2 tablespoons cold water

Preheat the oven to 200°C/180°C fan, and line two large baking sheets with greaseproof paper.

Put 330g of the nuts and seeds in a blender, and pulse until fine like flour. Pour the resulting mixture into a bowl, add the egg and cold water and mix until everything comes together into a stiff dough. If you need slightly more water, add it a teaspoon at a time – you don't want the dough to become too wet. Put the dough in the fridge for 30 minutes to chill.

Roll the chilled dough out between two sheets of greaseproof paper (to stop it sticking), to a thickness of around 0.5cm. Cut the dough into long triangles – this is easily done by slicing it into rectangles and scoring a diagonal line from one corner to the other – and place them 2cm apart on the baking sheets. Don't worry if they look a little rustic – I think it adds to their charm.

Wet your hands and lightly scatter water over the crackers. This will turn to steam in the oven and will help give them a crispy crust.

Take the remaining 20g of mixed nuts and seeds, chop finely and sprinkle on top. Bake for 25 minutes, swapping the baking sheets halfway through, until crisp. The nibbles will keep in an airtight tin for 3 to 4 days.

 TIP: *Use the saltiest nuts you can find for maximum flavour. Or, for a tasty kick, try chilli- or herb-coated nuts and seeds instead.*

CHEESY CRÊPES

EACH BATCH (2 CRÊPES) SERVES 1

Half pancake, half omelette, these light-as-a-feather crêpes make a super-easy midweek supper. I use low-fat cream cheese, but you can experiment with different varieties and flavours.

2 eggs	120g low-fat cream cheese	3 spring onions, finely chopped

Using a fork, lightly whisk the eggs and add 100g of the cream cheese, switching to a whisk if it doesn't combine easily. Stir until you have a smooth, pale batter. Add the spring onions to the batter, holding back a tablespoonful to serve. Allow the batter to stand for at least 30 minutes before cooking.

When it's ready, put a half teaspoon of oil in a frying pan over a medium heat. Test the heat of the pan by dropping a pea-sized amount of batter into the oil. If it sizzles, it's ready. As the batter is thin, you need the heat to be just right before you pour it in.

Using a ladle, add half the batter to the pan, cook for 2 to 3 minutes on one side, then flip (carefully) to cook the other side for the same amount of time. Repeat with the second half of the batter.

Arrange both crêpes on a plate, dollop the remaining cream cheese on top and sprinkle with the leftover spring onions. *Bon appétit!*

If you're making a batch for lots of people, simply multiply the ingredients. Two crêpes make an ample serving for one.

 TIP: *Swap the spring onions for any other veg or herbs – I like mushrooms, tomatoes and thinly sliced red peppers. If you want your crêpes really cheesy, you can even try a few handfuls of grated strong cheese, such as mature Cheddar or Parmesan.*

GOATS IN BLANKETS

MAKES 12 PIECES

Half pigs in blankets, half devils on horseback, these little cheese-stuffed, bacon-wrapped bites are perfect as a snack. You can use any soft cheese, but I like a medium-flavoured goat's cheese so it doesn't completely overpower the sweet dates.

6 rashers of smoked bacon – streaky or back, though streaky works better	100g soft goat's cheese	12 dates (big, plump Medjool ones if possible)

12 cocktail sticks

Preheat the oven to 220°C/200°C fan.

Cut each slice of bacon in half lengthways using a sharp knife.

Put the cheese in a bowl and whip it gently using a fork. This will soften it and make it easier to handle.

If the dates aren't pitted, remove the stones. Then slightly widen the hole in the centre of each using the back of a teaspoon – there needs to be room to pack lots of filling inside.

Stuff each date with a generous teaspoonful of cheese and wrap a strip of bacon around it, stretching it if you need to. Secure the bacon by pushing a cocktail stick right through the middle of the date.

Place the stuffed dates on a baking sheet and bake for 8 to 10 minutes, turning each one halfway through the cooking time.

Remove from the oven and place on kitchen paper for a minute to drain the fat off the bacon. You can eat the goats in blankets hot or cold, and they'll keep for a few days in the fridge.

PUDDINGS

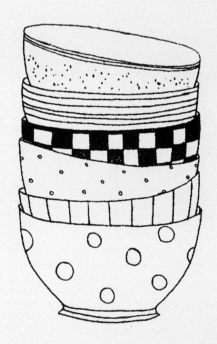

White choc cheesecake
Microwave meringues
Frozen key lime pie
Sticky syrup roly-poly
Lemon posset
Saucy maple fondants
Rhubarb crumble
Apple roses
Chocolate mousse
Yoghurt jelly pie
Raspberry ripple mousse
Cinnamon rice pud
Pain au chocolat pudding

WHITE CHOC CHEESECAKE

SERVES 8–10

More a soufflé than a cheesecake, this is my take on the light-as-a-cloud dessert that took the internet by storm a couple of years ago. It might not look like much of a showstopper, but it tastes like a giant marshmallow – so make enough to go around.

270g white chocolate	240g low-fat cream cheese, at room temperature	6 eggs

Medium round cake tin (23cm across)

Preheat the oven to 195°C/175°C fan, and line the sides and base of the cake tin with baking paper.

Melt 240g of the white chocolate in a heatproof bowl in 20-second bursts in the microwave, or over a pan of boiling water. Save the remaining 30g for later.

Add the cream cheese to the bowl and stir. If it's still lumpy, blast the bowl for another 10 seconds in the microwave so the cheese melts.

Separate the eggs, add the yolk to the cheese and chocolate mixture, and combine. In a separate bowl, whisk the egg whites until they form stiff peaks. It should take around 3 minutes with an electric mixer – or several more if you do it by hand.

Transfer the cheese and chocolate mixture to a much larger bowl – you'll need space to work. Slowly add spoonfuls of the egg white, stirring gently with a metal spoon as you go, until it's all combined. The mixture should be thick and pale. Keep going until all the lumps of egg white disappear, but don't over-mix – you want to keep as much air in there as possible.

Pour the cheesecake mixture into the cake tin. Set it in a baking tray and pour boiling water into the tray around the cake tin, around a third of the way up, to make a bain-marie.

Bake for 30 minutes, then switch the oven off and leave the cheesecake in there for another 10 minutes until it is spongy (rather than wobbly) to the touch. Let it cool completely in the tin before turning out. Don't worry if it sinks a little as it cools – it's so delicate that this is bound to happen.

Melt the remaining chocolate and drizzle it over the top of the cake. It should keep for up to a week in the fridge.

MICROWAVE MERINGUES

MAKES 15 LARGE MERINGUES

My mind was blown when I first came across this recipe, and it's taken me an age to get it just right. Baking purists might have a coronary, but I'm a convert. Watching the little white blobs puff up in the microwave is sheer magic – exactly what baking should be about.

280g icing sugar	30g egg white (roughly 2 medium eggs, or 1 large egg)	3 passion fruit or a punnet of fresh berries, to serve

Sift the icing sugar into the egg white and mix roughly with a wooden spoon (do not whisk). Using your hands, bring the mixture together into a ball. It should be the texture of thick paste. Knead until it is all combined and has an even texture throughout, then divide into walnut-sized balls (if you want to be precise, each should weigh around 20g).

Cut a circle of greaseproof paper to place over the turntable in the middle of the microwave.

Arrange two balls, well spaced out, on the paper. Heat in the microwave for 40 to 50 seconds, watching closely through the door. They should puff up but not touch one another. When they look big enough, stop the heat. If they need a little longer, add 5 seconds. In my 700W microwave (category D), they take exactly 60 seconds – but don't worry if yours is different. The key is to watch carefully what happens through the glass.

Remove the greaseproof paper from the microwave, allow the meringues to cool for a few minutes and place them on a wire rack. Repeat for the remainder of the batch. Serve drizzled with passion fruit seeds and juice for a tasty dessert, or crumble into whipped cream and berries to make an Eton mess.

Store in an airtight tin and they should keep for four or five days.

 TIP: *My brother-in-law calls these 'exploding meringues' – because if you drop them, they go EVERYWHERE. The intense heat makes them very fragile, so handle with care.*

FROZEN KEY LIME PIE

SERVES 8–10

A cheat's version of the classic American dessert, this tart combines a sweet, biscuity base with a zingy lime topping. You can make it several days before a dinner party and keep it in the freezer.

15 dark chocolate digestives (around 255g)	360g low-fat cream cheese	2 limes

Small round cake tin (20cm across)

Line the cake tin with baking paper.

Put 14 of the digestives in a heatproof bowl and microwave on high for 30 seconds. This will start to melt the chocolate, which helps bind the base together when it's in the tin. Blitz the digestives in a blender until they've turned to crumbs. Add 1 heaped teaspoon of cream cheese, just to help the mixture come together.

Pour into the cake tin and press down tightly with a spoon. Put in the fridge to chill.

In the meantime, put the cream cheese in a bowl and whip using a fork until it is light and fluffy.

Grate the zest of both limes. Squeeze the limes into the cream cheese, add half the lime zest and mix thoroughly.

Remove the biscuit base from the fridge, top with the cream cheese mixture and spread out with a rounded knife so the top is even. Crush the remaining digestive, mix it with the leftover lime zest and sprinkle over the top of the cheesecake.

Freeze for 3 to 4 hours, until the top is like ice cream.

Remove the pie from the freezer around 20 minutes before you want to serve it, and slice with a warmed knife. Once you've had your fill, cover the tin with cling film and put it back in the freezer. It should keep for at least a month.

STICKY SYRUP ROLY-POLY

This gooey pudding is my go-to comfort food: golden flaky pastry sitting in a bath of sweet, syrupy custard. It's so simple to make that you can do it between courses – as long as you don't mind getting your hands sticky. And yes, it contains an entire tin of golden syrup . . .

2 x 215g ready-rolled frozen puff pastry	420g golden syrup (1 full tin)	300ml semi-skimmed milk

Large rectangular crumble/lasagne dish (38cm x 25cm x 5cm)

Preheat the oven to 220°C/200°C fan, and prepare the dish by greasing it lightly with a little butter.

Allow the pastry rolls to completely defrost before unfurling each one into a flat rectangle.

Measure out the syrup into a jug. I grease mine with a little olive oil first – it stops the syrup from sticking and makes it easier to pour. Use a spatula to place the syrup evenly in the centre of each piece of pastry and spread it out until it sits around 2.5cm from each edge. Hold back a couple of teaspoons of syrup to pour on top.

Starting in the bottom left-hand corner, fold each pastry rectangle a few centimetres into the centre. Fold this edge into the centre again, and repeat until you have made two long diagonal rolls.

Gently lift the pastry rolls into the baking tray, using a fish slice for support, and lay them side by side but at a bit of a slant so they use the full length of the dish.

Pour the milk over the top of the rolls and drizzle on the remaining syrup.

Bake the roly-polies for 30 minutes, or until the pastry has puffed up and turned golden.

Serve straight from the dish, with dollops of crème fraîche.

LEMON POSSET

MAKES 6 POSSETS

These zesty little puds are my take on the classic posset – a medieval drink of curdled milk that has made a comeback as a modern-day dessert. You can make the possets well ahead of time and keep them in the fridge before serving.

2 x 284ml cartons of double cream	160g caster sugar	3 lemons

6 serving glasses, ramekins or small teacups

Prepare the serving glasses by placing them in the fridge to chill.

Put the cream and sugar in a saucepan over a medium heat. Whisk them together and bring to the boil slowly. Simmer for 2 to 3 minutes – the mixture should turn a rich yellow colour – before taking the pan off the hob.

While the mixture cools, grate the zest from all 3 lemons and squeeze the juice from 2. Add the juice and two-thirds of the zest to the cream mixture and whisk thoroughly until it is smooth.

Pour into the serving dishes and scatter the remaining zest on top.

Chill in the fridge for at least 3 hours before serving.

 TIP: *These taste great with a crunchy biscuit on the side – try a ginger biscuit, pistachio biscotti or one of my shortbread rounds (see page 20).*

SAUCY MAPLE FONDANTS

MAKES 4 FONDANTS

Fondant puddings are notoriously hard to make, but these ones are incredibly straightforward. The maple fondant centre is nutty, sweet and tangy all at the same time – just make sure you don't overcook them so it oozes out when you cut into them.

200g good-quality maple syrup	100g plain flour	4 eggs (2 whole eggs and 2 yolks)

4 ramekins or other small ovenproof dishes
Ice-cube tray

Prepare the ramekins by greasing them with a little butter and lining the base of each with a circle of greaseproof paper.

Pour 150g of the maple syrup into a bowl, sift in the flour and mix.

In a separate bowl, whisk the eggs and egg yolks together for a couple of minutes until they start to foam and turn pale. Add the eggs to the maple mixture and whisk to combine. Divide the mixture between the ramekins – they should be around two-thirds full – and place them in the fridge for 2 hours to set.

Meanwhile, spoon the remaining 50g of maple syrup into four squares of an ice-cube tray and place it in the freezer. They won't completely solidify, but the syrup will thicken and turn cloudy.

When you're ready to cook your fondants preheat the oven to 200°C/180°C fan. Remove the syrup ice cubes with a teaspoon and drop one into the centre of each ramekin mixture. Bake for 20 to 22 minutes (no more), or until the mixture is just set on top.

Scrape a knife around the inside edge of each ramekin to loosen the fondant, and turn it out on to a plate, tapping the bottom a few times if it's a little stuck. Do this quickly – you don't want them to keep cooking, or they'll harden up. Serve with whipped cream. Eat while hot to watch the syrupy centre flow out.

RHUBARB CRUMBLE

SERVES 6–8

This rough-and-ready classic warms the cockles on a cold day – and it's so easy to throw together. The sharpness of the rhubarb is offset by the sweet granola topping, held together with stick-in-your-teeth toffee. You can't beat it!

400g fresh rhubarb	100g caster sugar	200g your favourite granola (mine is apple, cinnamon and cherry)

Large rectangular crumble/lasagne dish (38cm x 25cm x 5cm)

Preheat the oven to 220°C/200°C fan.

Chop the rhubarb into 4cm-long chunks and place in the bottom of the crumble dish, sprinkled with half the sugar. Roast the rhubarb and sugar for 20 minutes.

Meanwhile, place the other half of the sugar in a heavy-bottomed saucepan over a low heat. Heat slowly until it caramelizes and turns golden brown. It should take roughly the same amount of time as the rhubarb does to roast – if it's going too quickly, turn the heat down.

Remove the rhubarb from the oven and add a few spoonfuls of juice from the dish to the caramelized sugar, stirring constantly so it doesn't stick.

Take the saucepan off the heat and add the granola. Mix thoroughly until most of it is coated and sticky. Scoop it out of the pan using a spatula and spread over the roasted rhubarb. (This can be quite a sticky job.) Pour any remaining sugar over the top of the crumble.

Bake for another 20 minutes, or until the topping is brown and the rhubarb bubbling. Enjoy with a side of ice cream – my cardamom custard flavour works a treat (see page 197).

TIP: *You can use dulce de leche, cinnamon sugar or raspberry conserve – or any other spread or curd you have to hand – instead of apricot jam.*

APPLE ROSES

Not only are these little pastry roses quick and easy to make, but they look and taste fantastic. Serve them with whipped cream for a dessert that's as pretty as a picture.

1 x 215g ready-rolled frozen puff pastry	3 red apples	6 tablespoons apricot jam

12-hole muffin tray

Preheat the oven to 200°C/180°C fan, and grease six holes of the muffin tray with plenty of butter.

Defrost the puff pastry and, once pliable, roll it out into a neat rectangle. Slice it into six long strips.

Core the apples, slice them in half and cut them from top to bottom into super-thin segments, no more than 2mm thick.

Put a blob of apricot jam in the centre of the first strip of pastry and spread it out to either end. Lay the apple segments lengthways along the top edge of the pastry strip, the flat side sitting on the pastry and the curved side hanging over the edge. Continue from one end to the other, slightly overlapping as you go. You should use around half an apple per pastry strip.

Starting at the same end you laid the first piece of apple, gently roll the pastry up into a cylinder, gathering in the jam and pieces of apple as you go. Secure with the other end of the pastry and place it, apple ends up, in a muffin case. Spread the apple pieces out slightly so they fill the case. Repeat for the other five roses. Brush any remaining jam over the tops to give them a shine.

Bake for around 45 minutes, or until the pastry is puffed and golden and the apples are just starting to singe. Use a spoon to take the roses out of the tray immediately (they can get stuck if you let them cool in there), and eat them while they're hot.

CHOCOLATE MOUSSE

MAKES 6 MINI MOUSSES

These little desserts are inspired by Heston Blumenthal's ingenious recipe. Even when you're making them you won't believe it's going to work – then suddenly, as if by magic, a mousse appears. Just don't tell anyone how simple it is; they'll think you've slaved away for hours.

300g chocolate (I like half milk and half dark, but you can use whichever you prefer)	170ml water	1 punnet of fresh raspberries (around 150g)

6 small ramekins or glass dishes

Roughly chop the chocolate into chunks. Place it (holding a few chunks back) in a saucepan along with the water and cook over a medium heat until all the chocolate has melted.

While the chocolate melts, make a cold bath by filling a large bowl with cold water (and ice if you have some) then placing a smaller bowl inside.

Pour the melted chocolate and water mixture into the smaller bowl. This chills it quickly, which is important for making your mousse light and fluffy.

Using an electric whisk – I really wouldn't recommend a hand whisk for this one – whisk the mousse for around 15 minutes on a high setting. It takes longer than you think so be patient, and you might want to cover the bowl with a tea towel for the first few minutes, as it can splatter everywhere.

The mousse is ready when it turns pale and creamy brown in colour and a dollop sits on the surface without sinking back into the mixture. Spoon it into the ramekins and smooth out the top of each mousse using a wet spoon.

Top with raspberries and the remaining chocolate chunks. *Et voilà!* The easiest chocolate mousse you'll ever make. You can eat the mousses immediately or chill them in the fridge until you're ready to serve.

TIP: *For a spicy kick, add a few shakes of dried chilli to the melted chocolate before whisking.*

YOGHURT JELLY PIE

175g digestive biscuits
(11–12 biscuits)

+

1 x 135g packet of
strawberry jelly cubes

+

340g low-fat
Greek yoghurt

YOGHURT JELLY PIE

SERVES 6–8

This silly, wobbly pie will quickly become a family favourite. Adding jelly to yoghurt not only makes it set like a cheesecake, but it gives it a zap of colour – this strawberry one turns a bright candy pink. Try experimenting with different flavours and make a jelly rainbow!

175g digestive biscuits (11–12 biscuits)	1 x 135g packet of strawberry jelly cubes	340g low-fat Greek yoghurt

Small round cake tin (20cm across)

Preheat the oven to 220°C/200°C fan. Line the bottom and sides of the cake tin with greaseproof paper. Make sure the paper fits exactly, as the jelly will mould to its shape. Put the digestive biscuits in a ziplock bag, make sure it's sealed and bash them into crumbs using a rolling pin. Take out a small handful of the mixture and set aside (this is to decorate the pie). Pour the rest into a big mixing bowl.

In a separate bowl, prepare the jelly according to the instructions on the packet – but don't add the cold water, just the boiling water. So you'll be adding half the liquid it tells you to.

Add 3 to 4 teaspoons of the concentrated jelly mixture to the biscuits to help bind them together. Tip them into the prepared tin and use a spoon to flatten them down and get rid of any gaps – you don't want any holes for the yoghurt to seep out. Bake the biscuit base for 10 minutes, then set aside to cool.

Add the yoghurt to the jelly and whisk until lump-free. Put the mixture in the fridge for 1 to 2 hours to thicken a little. Once it's reached the consistency of thick custard, pour the jelly over the base and put the pie in the fridge overnight to set.

When you're ready to serve, sprinkle the remaining biscuit crumbs over the top. Carefully remove the pie from the tin and slice into generous wedges, using a super-sharp knife dipped in boiling water to give a clean cut. Serve on its own or with handfuls of fruit to match your jelly flavour.

RASPBERRY RIPPLE MOUSSE

SERVES 4

Coconut cream (just like coconut milk but thicker and creamier) is a very versatile ingredient. It's runny if you use it straight from the cupboard, but chilling it in the fridge makes it gooey and mousse-like – ideal for making this brilliant berry pudding.

500ml coconut cream, chilled	1 punnet of fresh raspberries (around 150g)	1 x 12g sachet of gelatine

Large ceramic serving bowl

Plan ahead by chilling the coconut cream in the fridge overnight. You want to start with it nice and cold. Pour it into a bowl and whisk until smooth and frothy. This will take several minutes by hand, or 2 to 3 minutes with an electric whisk. Then place it back in the fridge. Put all but a small handful of the raspberries in a saucepan and heat slowly until the juice starts to bubble. Take the raspberries off the heat and use a fork to mash them through a sieve to create a smooth coulis.

Dissolve the gelatine sachet in hot water following the instructions on the packet. Add 40ml of the mixture to the coconut cream and whisk thoroughly. Don't worry if this thins it out – the gelatine will soon get to work doing the opposite.

Transfer your mousse to the serving bowl at this stage. I like to use one big, colourful bowl, but you can use individual ramekins, martini glasses or tumblers if you prefer. Place the mousse in the fridge to chill for 30 minutes – you want it to thicken up a little so the raspberries disperse. When it's a bit firmer, add the raspberries, a spoonful at a time, and gently swirl them through the mousse. Be careful not to over-mix: you want a visible ripple effect. Slice the remaining raspberries and scatter them over the top.

Place the mousse back in the fridge to set for at least 2 hours before serving. It's tangy rather than sweet, so it goes well with something rich – even just a handful of chopped chocolate sprinkled on top.

CINNAMON RICE PUD

SERVES 6

Rice pudding is my dad's favourite dessert – so no baking book would be complete without a tribute to him. This is a tricky one with three ingredients, as you can add all sorts of flavours and embellishments, but my secret ingredient is a nifty way of doing it all in one.

900ml semi-skimmed milk	130g pudding rice (or short-grain rice – it's the same thing)	160g cinnamon cereal (Golden Grahams, Curiously Cinnamon – or, to be honest, any wheat-based, flavoured cereal you want)

Deep pudding dish (capacity at least 2 litres)

Grease the base and sides of the pudding dish with a little butter.

Tip the milk into a saucepan and heat it gently until it just starts bubbling.

While it cooks, measure out the rice and crush 140g of the cereal by putting it in a ziplock bag and bashing it with a rolling pin. Don't turn it into crumbs – keeping a little bit of texture will give the pudding a nice crunch.

Take the milk off the heat, add the rice and cereal and give it all a stir. Let it infuse for a couple of minutes before pouring into the dish.

Bake your pudding for 1 hour, 20 minutes with the lid off. Check it after an hour – it should have a nice, golden skin on top and be bubbling around the edges. Serve the pudding straight from the dish, in big steaming spoonfuls topped with the remaining 20g of cereal, crumbled over the top.

 TIP: *Some people like their rice pudding runny – and this one is quite tightly packed. I like to have some extra hot milk on hand, so I can stir it in if I want.*

PAIN AU CHOCOLAT PUDDING

SERVES 8-10

This is a great way to use up stale or leftover pains au chocolat. Like a classic bread and butter pudding, it's sweet, stodgy and oh-so-bad for you. But nothing else quite hits the spot in the same way on a wintry afternoon – or after a slap-up Sunday lunch.

6 cooked pains au chocolat, cold	400ml double cream	4 eggs

Large rectangular crumble/lasagne dish (38cm x 25cm x 5cm)

Lightly grease the dish with a little butter or oil. Slice the cold pains au chocolat into four pieces and arrange them, chocolate filling side up, across the base of the dish. Pack them as tightly together as you can – try not to leave any gaps. There should be enough to cover the dish completely in a single layer, but if you have some leftovers, just squeeze them in between.

Pour the cream into a saucepan over a medium heat and heat it gently until it just starts to bubble (this shouldn't take more than 5 minutes).

In a separate bowl, lightly whisk the eggs with a fork. Once the cream is hot, add the eggs to the pan and whisk vigorously to combine. Immediately pour the custard over the pains au chocolat in the dish. Set aside for 40 minutes – you want the liquid to soak into the pastry, so the longer you leave it before baking, the better.

Preheat the oven to 200°C/180°C fan, and bake the pudding for 35 minutes until golden, puffed up and bubbling with eggy custard. Serve hot. Sprinkle lemon zest over the top for a fancy finish, if you like.

 TIP: *This tastes delicious drizzled with my Auntie Sarah's Mars bar sauce – another three-ingredient recipe. Heat 3 chopped Mars bars in a saucepan with 120ml of water and half a teaspoon instant coffee. Whisk together until the chocolate melts and the sauce thickens.*

ICE CREAM
AND SORBET

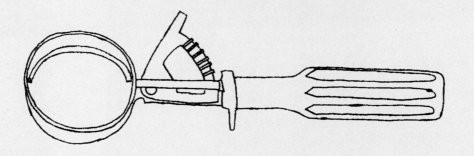

Coffee ice cream
Lemon blueberry lollies
Peanut banana ice
Fizzy orange sherbets
Banoffee cake pops
Coconut ice cream
Peach melba sorbet
Retro Viennetta
Very berry sorbet
Ice cream float pops
Avo ice lollies
Cardamom custard ice cream
Nutella mini milks

COFFEE ICE CREAM

SERVES 6

My mum adores coffee ice cream, so this is for her – a smooth, creamy dessert that will not only give you a caffeine kick but will keep you cool and refreshed on a summery day.

1 espresso (3 teaspoons instant coffee mixed with 2 teaspoons boiling water)	200g sweetened condensed milk (roughly ½ a tin)	610g evaporated milk (roughly 1½ tins)

1-litre freezer-safe plastic container

Clean and dry the container and line it with cling film. You need enough to cover the edges and completely seal the top. This will help with serving the ice cream later.

Make the espresso in a mug and allow it to cool slightly. Pour the condensed milk into a big bowl and stir in the espresso.

Taste the ice cream at this stage – I'm a bit of a wuss when it comes to coffee, but some people might like it stronger. Add another teaspoon of espresso if you want.

Pour the evaporated milk into the bowl. Whisk the mixture for 5 to 6 minutes using the highest setting on your electric whisk, until it's bubbly and pale in colour. Tip the ice cream into the tub, fold the cling film over the top and seal the lid.

Freeze for 3 hours, then take it out and stir it through (this stops ice crystals from forming) before putting it back in the freezer for another 3 hours, or overnight.

Take the ice cream out 20 minutes before serving to make it easier to scoop. It should keep in the freezer for a few months.

ICE CREAM AND SORBET

LEMON BLUEBERRY LOLLIES

MAKES 8 LOLLIES

These are a funky alternative to shop-bought fruit lollies – and they're not only healthy but incredibly moreish. You can substitute the blueberries for any berry and experiment with different yoghurts. I like raspberries with a swirl of tangy apple flavour, too.

1 punnet of fresh blueberries (around 200g)	1 tablespoon semi-skimmed milk	600g tub of sweetened lemon yoghurt

8-hole plastic lolly mould – whatever shape you prefer
Wooden lolly sticks or plastic holders

Start by cleaning and drying the lolly moulds and sticks.

Put the berries in a saucepan and heat for around 5 minutes over a medium heat until they start to bubble. Allow to cool slightly before adding the milk and blending, by hand or using a mixer, until only a few chunks of berries remain.

Tip the lemon yoghurt into a bowl and add the cooled blueberry mixture. Stir lightly, not mixing through, to create a marbled effect.

Spoon the lolly mixture carefully into the moulds and place them in the freezer. Fill each one around three-quarters full so they don't overflow as they freeze.

Leave for at least 5 hours – or preferably overnight – before eating.

PEANUT BANANA ICE

SERVES 6

Bananas make a healthy ice cream base – and blending them with peanut butter turns them into a delicious iced dessert. I like to add chopped peanuts, really salty ones, which give a satisfying crunch and stop it all from becoming too sweet.

4 ripe bananas, peeled	340g smooth peanut butter (an average-sized jar)	100g salted peanuts

500ml freezer-safe plastic container

Line the sides and base of the container with cling film so there's enough to cover the top of the ice cream once it's set.

Purée the bananas in a blender until smooth. Slowly add the peanut butter, blending it with the bananas in between each addition. If you add it all in one go, it can stick together in a clump.

Add two-thirds of the peanuts, and stir them in by hand. Tip the ice cream into the container and flatten out the top. Scatter the remaining peanuts on top.

Freeze for around 4 hours for a soft-serve ice cream, or 6 hours for a harder-set scoop.

FIZZY ORANGE SHERBETS

MAKES 6 LOLLIES

Remember sherbet Dip Dabs? Well, this is the ice cream equivalent – fizzy, juicy orange lollies that taste good and will keep the kids happy when the sun shines.

500ml orange juice (with or without bits – your choice)	30g caster sugar	1½ teaspoons bicarbonate of soda

6-hole plastic lolly mould – whatever shape you prefer
Wooden lolly sticks or plastic holders

Clean and dry the lolly moulds and sticks.

Measure the orange juice out into a large jug, then add the caster sugar and whisk thoroughly.

Now for the fun bit . . . Add the bicarbonate of soda, a little bit at a time, and watch as the mixture fizzes and bubbles like a magic potion. The more you whisk it, the more it'll expand – so be careful not to let it overflow.

Taste the sherbet mixture – if it's too sweet, add a little more orange juice, or a spoon more sugar if it's bitter.

Leave for 15 to 20 minutes to let the fizzing subside, before decanting into the lolly moulds, filling them around three-quarters full (remember, the liquid will expand as it freezes).

Depending on the size of your moulds, there should be enough for 6 to 8 lollies.

Freeze for at least 4 hours – and save the lollies for a balmy afternoon.

BANOFFEE ICE CREAM POPS

MAKES 18 TINY CAKE POPS

Like a frozen banoffee pie, these tiny ice cream pops are the perfect party food. Adding dulce de leche, a rich South American toffee sauce, makes them an indulgent treat – but the bananas and yoghurt keep them (vaguely) healthy at the same time.

1 ripe banana, peeled	75g dulce de leche (or other thick toffee sauce)	125g low-fat Greek yoghurt

3 x 6-hole silicone cake-pop moulds, Cake-pop sticks or round wooden skewers, Piping bag and super-fine nozzle

Mash the banana to a pulp in a bowl. Stir in the dulce de leche and yoghurt, and mix thoroughly until well combined. I like to leave a few chunks of banana – but you can keep stirring if you want it completely smooth.

Clean and dry your cake-pop moulds (or one small tub if you prefer to eat it like regular ice cream) and sticks. If you're using skewers, you'll need to cut them down to around 12cm long. Use a teaspoon to tease the mixture in the top and bottom half of the moulds, then attach them together. You'll need to work fast so the mixture doesn't squidge out the sides. Once the moulds are attached, put any remaining mixture in the piping bag and squirt it through the hole in the top of each mould to ensure they're completely full.

Freeze for at least 3 hours, or preferably overnight. When you're ready to serve, remove the moulds from the freezer for 10 minutes so the ice cream softens. Push a stick halfway into each ice cream pop through the hole in the mould and return them to the freezer to set for another 10 minutes.

Pop them out and serve arranged in a jam jar or with the sticks poked into a skin-on banana.

 TIP: *These taste delicious dipped in chocolate and sprinkles – like an old-school Fab lolly. Coat in cooled, melted dark chocolate and dip in multicoloured vermicelli for a fun finish.*

COCONUT ICE CREAM

SERVES 6–8

OK, so it's not technically an ice cream – more of an iced cream, as it doesn't have a custard base. But this light, tropical slice of paradise will transport you straight to the Caribbean. All you need now is a piña colada and a cocktail umbrella on the side.

2 x 400ml tins of coconut milk, chilled	325g caster sugar	2 teaspoons vanilla extract

Standard loaf tin (22cm x 12cm x 7cm) or 1-litre freezer-safe plastic container

Store the coconut milk in the fridge, preferably overnight, before making this. Keeping it cold will help kick-start the process once it goes into the freezer.

Line the loaf tin or container with several layers of cling film, overlapping the edges a few times so there is an extra flap large enough to cover the top of the ice cream once it fills the tin. You'll also use this flap to slide the ice cream out before serving.

Pour the coconut milk into a large bowl and whisk until it forms a smooth, bubbly mixture. Add the sugar, whisk thoroughly, and repeat with the vanilla extract.

Pour the mixture into the lined tin and cover the top with the flaps of cling film. Place in the lowest part of the freezer (where it will be coldest), and leave for 30 minutes. Remove the ice cream, whisk it through in the tin and replace in the freezer. Repeat this every half-hour at least six times – then leave the ice cream to set.

The repeated whisking does the job of an ice cream maker – putting as much air as possible into the mix. This stops crunchy ice crystals from forming and spoiling the even texture.

It should take another 3 hours to freeze, though it will never go quite as solid as a shop-bought ice cream. On the plus side, this makes it easier to scoop and serve.

The ice cream will keep for up to 2 months in the freezer.

PEACH MELBA SORBET

SERVES 6-8

Half sorbet, half slushie, this peachy pud is sweet and refreshing – and, as it gets all its creaminess from the yoghurt, so much better for you than Ben & Jerry's . . .

6 whole peaches (or around 2 x 415g tins if you prefer)	4 dessert spoons runny honey	220g Greek yoghurt

500ml freezer-safe plastic container

Clean and dry the container and set it aside.

Peel, de-stone and cut the peaches in half. Alternatively, if using tinned fruit, drain off the liquid. Put the peach halves into a food processor along with the honey, and blitz until smooth. Add the yoghurt, and repeat.

When the mixture is completely lump-free, decant into the container and freeze for 5 hours or overnight, until set. You don't need to churn or mix it throughout – the texture is supposed to be quite icy, so don't worry if a few crystals form.

Allow the sorbet to soften at room temperature for 20 minutes or so before serving. Enjoy topped with flaked almonds or raspberry coulis.

RETRO VIENNETTA

As a child, this was my favourite pudding. I loved the combination of creamy vanilla with the crispy chocolate. My version uses soured cream to give a sharper tang to the ice cream, and super-sweet chocolate-dipped wafers for the layers in between.

440ml soured cream	1 x 397g tin of sweetened condensed milk	250g chocolate-dipped wafers (such as Kit Kats or Tunnock's caramel wafers)

Standard loaf tin (22cm x 12cm x 7cm)

Prepare the loaf tin by lining it with greaseproof paper. You want the edges to be as straight as possible, so keep it neat – and make sure there's enough overhang to cover the top and seal the ice cream in once you've finished.

Whisk the soured cream and condensed milk together until smooth. Chop each of the wafers in half horizontally to make long, thin rectangles. If they're still quite thick (it depends on the brand you're using), chop them in half again. Starting at the bottom of the tin, place the wafer pieces in a neat layer so they completely cover the base. Treat it like a jigsaw, plugging any gaps with wafer so it's fixed in place. Pour in a layer of cream and place in the freezer for an hour to firm up.

Repeat with another layer of wafer pieces and cream, and re-freeze. Keep repeating this step until you have enough left for one final layer. This time, take it out of the freezer and pour the cream on first. Then decorate the top with the remaining wafer pieces, finely chopped.

Put the Viennetta in the freezer for at least 6 hours or overnight, to set completely.

When you're ready to serve, let it soften for 20 minutes before removing from the tin. Pull the greaseproof paper gently up from the ends and sides so as not to rip it, and slice the Viennetta into chunky wedges using a serrated knife. Deeeeelish!

VERY BERRY SORBET

SERVES 6–8

Frozen berries are a godsend – I always keep a packet in my freezer for making smoothies, topping puddings or turning into this easy-as-pie sorbet. I use egg whites in mine, which thickens it and makes it last longer, but you can always leave them out if you prefer.

500g frozen mixed berries	100g granulated sugar	2 egg whites

1-litre freezer-safe plastic container

Clean and dry the ice cream container. You don't need to line it, as the sorbet is nice and easy to scoop out.

Heat the berries in a saucepan with 30g of the sugar for around 20 minutes, over a low heat, until they soften. Take them off the heat and mash them with a potato masher to squash any remaining whole berries. Don't worry about getting it completely smooth; I quite like it chunky. Pour the mixture into the ice cream container and freeze for an hour.

Meanwhile, whisk the egg whites into soft peaks, add the rest of the sugar and whisk again so it's all combined (just like a runny meringue).

When the frozen berries are ready – ice crystals should have just started to form – take them out of the freezer and stir in the egg mixture. You can mix it thoroughly so it's all one colour or leave a few ripples – the rich purple tones are lovely.

Return the container to the freezer for at least 4 hours, stirring twice during the first hour to stop it becoming too icy.

Scoop and serve, scattered with fresh mint if you like.

ICE CREAM FLOAT POPS

MAKES 6 POPS

Ice cream floats were my ultimate childhood treat. I remember being mesmerized by the fizzy, gurgling bubbles that formed as the creamy ice cream bobbed around in my glass, and slurping the foam off the top. I've tried to recreate that magic in these float pops.

6 teaspoons popping candy	500ml vanilla ice cream	400ml cola

6 disposable polystyrene or plastic cups
Wooden lolly sticks

Put half a teaspoon of popping candy in the bottom of each cup. Make a float by adding a tablespoon of ice cream to each, followed by a glug of cola (around 200ml should be enough for all six cups). The mixture will fizz and pop as the ingredients combine. Give it a quick stir, and place in the freezer for an hour.

While the first layer sets, leave the vanilla ice cream out of the freezer to go runny.

Next, remove the pops from the freezer. Carefully insert the sticks into the middle of each mould, pushing down almost to the bottom, and add another half teaspoon of popping candy. Fill each cup up to two-thirds full with the remainder of the ice cream, making sure to level it out and clean around the inside edge with a piece of kitchen roll – you want nice, clean lines. Put the pops back in the freezer to set.

After another hour, take them out and fill almost to the brim with the remainder of the cola. Re-freeze for another 3 hours.

Run the outside of each cup under a hot tap for 10 seconds to release the pops – and, if you need to, simply cut away the paper cup. If you want one final kick, roll them in popping candy before eating. Prepare to have your taste buds tickled!

 TIP: *If you can't find popping candy, use something else zingy – like finely chopped, crystallized ginger – to perk these ice pops up. And you can replace the cola with any fizzy drink you fancy.*

AVO ICE LOLLIES

MAKES 6 LOLLIES

Avocados have been the most fashionable veg around for a couple of years now – ironic, really, because they're actually a fruit. Blending them with condensed milk and cocoa turns them into a healthy but delicious-tasting dessert that freezes well.

2 ripe avocados	300g sweetened condensed milk (roughly ¾ of a tin)	3 tablespoons cocoa powder

6-hole plastic lolly mould – whatever shape you prefer
Wooden lolly sticks or plastic holders

Clean and dry the lolly moulds and sticks.

Peel and de-stone the avocados and put them in a blender. Blitz on high for 30 seconds, until a smooth green paste forms. Add the condensed milk, a spoonful at a time, and keep blending until it's all combined.

Tip the mixture out of the blender and into a bowl containing the cocoa powder. Stir everything together until it turns a rich brown colour.

Spoon the mixture into the lolly moulds, banging them down hard on a table top every couple of spoons to get rid of any air bubbles. You want the moulds around three-quarters full (remember, the mixture will expand as it freezes).

Place in the freezer and leave for at least 6 hours to set.

 TIP: *If you don't have time to freeze the lollies, pour the mixture into ramekins instead of moulds, chill in the fridge and serve them as chocolate mousse pots.*

CARDAMOM CUSTARD ICE CREAM

This delicately spiced ice cream is the perfect accompaniment to a fruity summer dessert, or on the side of something stodgier (like my rhubarb crumble, see page 165). The custard base is sweet and comforting, while the cardamom gives it an exotic kick.

400ml semi-skimmed milk	6 cardamom pods	2 teaspoons custard powder

500ml freezer-safe plastic container

Clean and dry the container and line it with cling film – enough to overlap the sides and top to seal the ice cream in.

Put the milk in a saucepan, then add the cardamom pods and heat slowly over a medium heat to allow the flavour to infuse. Let it simmer for 5 to 10 minutes.

Meanwhile, put the custard powder in a large bowl, add a few tablespoons of the milk from the saucepan and mix to form a paste. Once the milk is ready, pour it over the custard paste, stirring constantly. Return the mixture to the saucepan and heat gently until it starts to thicken.

At this point, remove it from the heat, fish out the cardamom pods and use an electric whisk to beat it until it is light and fluffy. Allow the foam to settle before decanting into the ice cream tub.

Place on the lowest shelf of the freezer and leave for half an hour. Remove the ice cream, stir and put it back in the freezer. Repeat this every 30 minutes, at least six times. It's a faff, but it will stop ice crystals from ruining the creamy texture.

Leave for another 3 hours before serving in scoops.

NUTELLA MINI MILKS

MAKES 12 MINI MILKS OR 6 NORMAL-SIZED LOLLIES

These lollies take me right back. They come in boxes of three flavours – vanilla, chocolate and strawberry – and I used to fight with my siblings over who got the chocolate ones. My version, made with coconut cream, is devilishly indulgent.

225g coconut cream, chilled	150g Nutella (just under half a jar)	90g dark chocolate

2 x 6-hole plastic mini milk moulds – or 1 normal 6-hole lolly mould
Wooden lolly sticks or plastic holders

Chill the coconut cream in the fridge overnight so it starts the process nice and cold.

Next, clean and dry the lolly moulds and sticks. Lightly grease the insides of the moulds using a little sunflower oil (this is to help slide the lollies out later).

Put the coconut cream in a blender with the Nutella and whiz on high for a few minutes.

In the meantime, melt the chocolate in a small heatproof bowl in the microwave, in 20-second bursts, or over a saucepan of boiling water. Let the chocolate cool slightly before adding it to the other ingredients and blending them all together.

Pour the lolly mixture into the moulds – it should go around three-quarters up the sides to leave room for expansion – and freeze them overnight.

When it comes to getting your mini milks out, they can be a little stubborn, so run the moulds under the hot tap for 20 seconds and they should soon release.

 TIP: *For an alcoholic kick, swap the dark chocolate for a slug of Baileys liqueur. Adults only!*

ACKNOWLEDGEMENTS

I owe a lot of people a lot of thank yous. So, in no particular order, a huge thanks from the very bottom of my heart to . . .

Mum, Dad, Anna and David. Thank you for putting up with me waffling on about three-ingredient baking for what feels like years; Mum and Anna in particular for giving up countless afternoons to test recipes; David and Dad for happily scoffing whatever was put in front of them. Your love, support and unwavering encouragement got me through the tough bits. I don't think anyone loves food as much as the Raineys – and long may it continue. You're the best.

Grandma, for making sure a love of baking was deeply ingrained in me from the start. I hope I've done your recipes proud – and that you're looking down, watching all this with a smile.

The Hiltons, my fantastic family-in-law, for trying out some of my stranger creations along the way. You've been so kind and supportive – and I'm forever grateful. We're still finding bits of the exploding meringues around the house.

Sam Panday, for your endless enthusiasm for this book, that equally endless appetite and your creative ideas for the title. If there's ever a sequel, you know exactly what it'll be called.

The brilliant Clare Hulton, without whose instant enthusiasm, hard work and genuine passion for the idea this project would never have got off the ground.

Laurie Perry, without a doubt THE best food stylist and baker extraordinaire, who made my humble cakes and biscuits look like works of art. You're inspiring, amazing at what you do and you have fabulous taste in skirts.

The great Al Richardson, astrophysics genius-turned-photographer, whose patience, eye for detail and all-round excellence are truly humbling. Thank you for your stunning photographs, the many hundreds of miles of driving, and brightening up every day on the shoot with your colourful tales from Portugal.

All the lovely people (currently and formerly) at Penguin – Zoe Berville, Daniel Bunyard, Sarah Fraser, James Blackman, Ione Walder, Katie Bowden, Jenny Platt. And above all Lindsey Evans. It was a privilege to work with you and to spend time with your beautiful family. Thank you for letting us into your home, for feeding and watering us, for those many trips to the corner shop, for lending me your clothes – and for saying yes to this idea and turning my little dream into a reality.

My work colleagues, both past and present, for your interest and excitement about this book, for tasting my creations and for not minding (too much) when I took days off to work on it. You know who you are. A huge special thank you to Fiona Hardcastle, for always being there. And to Mikey's colleagues, too, for eating tins and tins of leftovers, wonky biscuits and not-too-sure-about-the-flavour cakes. Your feedback has been invaluable.

And last, the biggest thank you of all to Mikey, my wonderfully supportive husband, who has put up with me dusting our entire house with icing sugar, clogging the sink with crumbs, filling the fridge with ingredients and covering every available surface with a Jenga tower of cake tins. You've put up with more three-ingredient dinners than I deserve. You've feigned enjoyment even with the ones that tasted like feet. You're probably more relieved than I am that this is over – but without you I would never have got here.

Three little words: I love you.

INDEX

Page references in **bold** indicate an illustration

MICHAEL JOSEPH

UK | USA | Canada | Ireland | Australia
India | New Zealand | South Africa

Michael Joseph is part of the Penguin Random House group of companies
whose addresses can be found at global.penguinrandomhouse.com.

First published 2018
003

Set in Brandon Text and Caecilia LT Std
Colour reproduction by Rhapsody Ltd, London
Printed in Italy

A CIP catalogue record for this book is available from the British Library

ISBN: 978-0-718-18479-7

www.greenpenguin.co.uk

MIX
Paper from
responsible sources
FSC® C018179

Penguin Random House is committed to a
sustainable future for our business, our readers
and our planet. This book is made from Forest
Stewardship Council® certified paper.